"This is a powerful and passi and wonderfully humble. This recover hope and courage. It will ....others. And most important, this book ..... help you find a deeper life in Jesus."

—John Eldredge, author of *Wild at Heart* and *Beautiful Outlaw*

"You may desire to be a great businessman, which is a noble goal. But there is an even higher calling—to be a good man for the kingdom of God. *No Matter the Cost* should be required reading for anyone who is fighting to be such a good man."

—Tommy Spaulding, business consultant and *New York Times* bestselling author of *It's Not Just Who You Know*

"This is a book filled not with bravado but with stories of men 'limping home, barely brave.' Vance's storytelling and John's golden pen result in a feast of all that is possible when men are willing to admit their need to live honestly before other men. The men I respect the most desire and live this."

—Jan Meyers Proett, counselor, speaker, author of *The Allure of Hope* and *Listening to Love*

"Vance Brown has given us the spiritual weapons we need to become better fathers, husbands, and ministry leaders. His writing is heartfelt and his message is clear: God is calling all men to engage in a battle—the fight of our lives, the struggle we were created for. *No Matter the Cost* is a battle cry for authentic manhood."

—Arnie Cole, CEO of Back to the Bible and coauthor of *Unstuck*

"This book is a uniquely authentic call to the deepest part of a man's soul. Anyone in whom God's Spirit is moving will respond. The results could be dramatic."

—Dr. Larry Crabb, founder of NewWay Ministries

"Vance Brown leads us on a journey that has more twists and turns than straight and level ground, but the view he leads us to see is so breathtaking that it is worth the long arduous hike. Walk with Vance and come to see the spectacular beauty of the One who has been with you in the defeats and the sweet respites. This book invites the heart to hope again."

—Dan B. Allender, PhD, professor of counseling psychology and founding president, The Seattle School of Theology and Psychology

"This book is a cry for men to live the life for which they were created, a call to live a life of significance that I too encourage you to consider."

—Bob Buford, author of *Halftime* and *Finishing Well*

"*No Matter the Cost* issues a radical challenge to men of all ages: Become the Christ-built warriors we were created to be—unbending in faith, unselfish in attitude, always honorable, and humble in word and deed. Every man must hear Vance Brown's powerful message and then pass it on to the next generation."

—Michael Ross, bestselling author of *What Your Son Isn't Telling You*

"Through *No Matter the Cost*, Vance challenges and encourages us as men to know who we are! He provides insight into God's Word and shares amazing stories that will challenge us to get in the fight, no matter the cost!"

—Dave Dravecky, former Major League Baseball player and president and founder of Endurance with Jan and Dave Dravecky

NO
MATTER
THE
COST

NO
MATTER
THE
COST

VANCE BROWN
WITH JOHN BLASE

BETHANY HOUSE PUBLISHERS

a division of Baker Publishing Group
Minneapolis, Minnesota

© 2012 by We Happy Few, Inc.

Published by Bethany House Publishers
11400 Hampshire Avenue South
Bloomington, Minnesota 55438
www.bethanyhouse.com

Bethany House Publishers is a division of
Baker Publishing Group, Grand Rapids, Michigan

Printed in the United States of America

Library of Congress Cataloging-in-Publication Data

Brown, Vance.
    No matter the cost / Vance Brown with John Blase.
        p. cm.
    Summary: "A successful entrepreneur and ministry leader calls men to band together and embrace a larger vision of Christian purpose. Presents biblical insights and stories aimed at living a meaningful life. Includes a small-group discussion guide"—Provided by publisher.
    ISBN 978-0-7642-0999-4 (pbk. : alk. paper)
    1. Christian men—Religious life. I. Blase, John. II. Title.
BV4528.2.B77 2012
248.8'42—dc23   2012001916

Unless otherwise indicated, Scripture quotations are from the Holy Bible, New International Version®. NIV®. Copyright © 1973, 1978, 1984, 2011 by Biblica, Inc.™ Used by permission of Zondervan. All rights reserved worldwide. www.zondervan.com

Scripture quotations identified ESV are from The Holy Bible, English Standard Version® (ESV®), copyright © 2001 by Crossway, a publishing ministry of Good News Publishers. Used by permission. All rights reserved. ESV Text Edition: 2007

Scripture quotations identified THE MESSAGE are from The Message by Eugene H. Peterson, copyright © 1993, 1994, 1995, 2000, 2001, 2002. Used by permission of NavPress Publishing Group. All rights reserved.

Scripture quotations identified NASB are from the New American Standard Bible®, copyright © 1960, 1962, 1963, 1968, 1971, 1972, 1973, 1975, 1977, 1995 by The Lockman Foundation. Used by permission.

Scripture quotations identified NKJV are from the New King James Version. Copyright © 1982 by Thomas Nelson, Inc. Used by permission. All rights reserved.

Scripture quotations identified NLT are from the Holy Bible, New Living Translation, copyright © 1996, 2004, 2007 by Tyndale House Foundation. Used by permission of Tyndale House Publishers, Inc., Carol Stream, Illinois 60188. All rights reserved.

Scripture quotations identified KJV are from the King James Version of the Bible.

Any Internet addresses (websites, blogs, etc.) used in this book are provided as a resource. Baker Publishing Group does not vouch for their content for the life of this book, nor do they imply an endorsement by Baker Publishing Group.

Cover design by Faceout Studio/Jeff Miller

Author is represented by Alive Communications, Inc.

12 13 14 15 16 17 18   7 6 5 4 3 2 1

This is a book for the barely brave
who've lived long enough to know
the texture of pain,
the smell of defeat,
the sound of loneliness,
the sight of betrayal,
and the taste of discouragement.
It is a book for broken men
who've come to their senses
and are limping toward home,
refusing to give up no matter the cost.

This book is dedicated to the most important person of my life—my wife: I love you, Betsy. Thank you for forgiving me. Your wisdom and beauty are captivating. You are precious to me. I look forward to getting old with you!

Contents

Foreword

This book has stirred up something in me that will never be the same again. My wife, Shaunti, and I have known Vance Brown for years and were delighted when he approached us about writing the foreword. But we were absolutely unprepared to be rocked by the power of this message—and by the overwhelming feeling that God is using these pages to awaken something in millions of men who instinctively know that they are called to be part of a larger story.

Every man dreams of being great—or at least we did when we were young and had a wide-open future. We dream of being a great athlete, great businessman, great thinker, great husband, great dad. We want to be men of valor, of courage; men who protect the ones we love and who accomplish something that matters with our lives. Yet at the same time, every man I know, every man in our research, secretly questions whether he has what it takes. It is easy to allow our self-doubts and the challenges of life to press in on us, diminish us, reduce us to settling for something other than the high calling we once thought we were supposed to achieve.

Maybe, we think, we are foolish to believe we are made for something more.

This book shines a spotlight inside the deepest, most important desires of our hearts as men, and shows us that those desires are not only acceptable and right—they are what we are built for. This book shows us that it has never been more imperative for us to pursue the high callings God has set before us, no matter the cost.

Yes, we are imperfect and broken, and many of us have made foolish, even life-altering mistakes; yet in these pages you will find other imperfect, broken, foolish men . . . who have become great warriors in the battle of our time. In these pages you will see stories of their trials, sufferings, and failures. You will see that their mingled feelings of confusion and latent courage, inadequacy and resolve are just like ours. This book gave me comfort and hope as I read some of these tales and found the common denominators for coming out on the other side: trust in our Father's plan and goodness—and being simply unwilling to quit.

The name of Vance's ministry, Band of Brothers, originates from the stirring words of Shakespeare in his play (and the movie) *Henry V*, as he imagined what King Henry V might have said to his troops before the Battle of Agincourt in 1415. The English were weakened, sick, and demoralized, facing impossible odds in the battle to defeat the French, who were blocking their route home. The king's cousin, Westmoreland, laments aloud the wish for more men, but the king will hear none of it. Instead, he calls the troops he does have together with a powerful call to courage and brotherhood, ending with the famous words, "We few, we happy few, we band of brothers; for he today that sheds his blood with me shall be my brother." Shortly thereafter comes the news that the

French are charging, and the previously quaking Westmoreland cries out in readiness, "Perish the man whose mind is backward now!"

The king asks, "Thou dost not wish more help from England, coz?"

Westmoreland shouts, "God's will! My liege, would you and I alone, without more help, could fight this royal battle!"

What turned a group of demoralized, broken men facing daunting odds into men that ended up routing their enemies and, indeed, winning this vital battle? The leadership of their king, the fellowship with their brothers, and the call to great courage and action at a pivotal time.

That is the message of this book. Today we have a King who is calling each of us to great courage, great action, together. He is calling us to look beyond the visible and see the great battle that is taking place in our world today—a fight and a stand to which the men of God are called, regardless of what comes.

Every man wants to be those men of greatness. And, as Shaunti puts it, every woman wants today's men to rise up and become those men of greatness as well.

We live in challenging times, and like Vance, I believe the battle for our world, our nation, and our families will only grow more intense in the season ahead. We need men who won't give up, no matter the cost. May you, may I, be a part of that Band of Brothers.

—Jeff and Shaunti Feldhahn
entrepreneurs, social researchers,
and bestselling authors of
For Men Only and *For Women Only*

Acknowledgments

Pete Gannon and Matt Dealy, thank you for fighting side by side with me in this ministry called Band of Brothers. This book has the message and charge God has given *us*. It has been my honor to serve and journey together with you good men. Brent Curtis, to me you are the "father" of our Band of Brothers ministry. Thanks for believing in me. Looking forward to seeing you and sharing stories on the other side. Keith Brown, what an honor it is to be your brother in Christ and blood brother. What an awesome redemptive story we have together. Satan didn't win! Philip Brown, another blood brother, you are not crazy—I also believe we are in the end moments. Never stop singing your song. Tim and Karen Pfeifer, I am so grateful that my children have had a second home. Tim, you are a dear brother and business partner. Karen, thank you for your prophetic letter to me twelve years ago that introduced me to Revelation 12:11. I am also grateful to Mark Beamer, Cris Child, Britt Jones, Jim Kretchman, Aaron McHugh, Steve Metcalf, Mark Morris, Matt Neigh, Tim Oakley, and Pete Ohlin. It is awesome to experience true Jonathan-David friendships and prove that they can exist in these days!

I also want to thank my children and parents: Collin, even though you are young, through your valiant battle with cancer, you taught me more about courage and faith than anyone I know. We experienced a Rite of Passage together. Noelle, you will always be my little girl, my delight—my princess. You are strong and determined like Eowyn. No one should underestimate you, because God is with you. Dylan, you are a mighty warrior who will always "get back up"—I see it in you. Your lens for truth is way beyond your years. I am so proud of you. Thanks to my parents, Brevard and Doris Brown. I truly am grateful for your love, sacrifices, and prayers.

I want to thank my coauthor-brother (in spite of what the cover says) and my agent-brother: John Blase, you are an anointed warrior-poet. Thanks for giving me the verses to sing my song. Rick Christian, this book would never have happened but for you. Thank you for believing in this project and in me. Your kingdom impact is far-reaching—I've witnessed over the years how well you fight and how God rewards you for it!

And I want to thank some of the men in my Band of Brothers: Thanks to other brothers who have covered my back consistently over the years through the *test of time* in this journey of sanctification. I love you, men: Bill Bantz, David Bervig, Sam Bhatt, Gary Birkhead, Eric Carlson, Rick Clapp, Dave Dravecky, Jeff Feldhahn, Arlen Feldman, Sam Froggatte, Craig Glass, Mike Henshaw, Ben Horton, Jesse Jones, Jeff Kiepke, Dave Kolb, Don Lacasse, Stuart Lundh, Gary Mellott, Mike St. Marie, Chadd Miller, Kent Miller, Bob Mills, Rick Mueller, Ron Muns, Greg Murtha, Leo Navarrete, Ed Pepping, Tony Probert, Steve Proett, Bill Ragsdale,

Brandon Ragsdale, Rusty Ray, Paul Reilly, Wes Roberts, Chuck Schwartz, Jurg Seyffer, Morgan Snyder, Steve Smith, Michael Thompson, Dan Vanada, Russell Verhey, Jeff Weeks, Taft Wennik, Kelly Williams, and Mike Worley.

Finally, thanks to the brothers in my band who also wielded their swords in powerful and beautiful ways in producing and editing the book and the supplemental video materials. *Audio-visual*: Pete Gannon, Britt Jones, and Stephen Vidano. *Editing and marketing*: Jeff Braun, Mark Chambers, and Carra Carr.

Last but not least, thank you to the mentors throughout my life, either personally or through their writings and lifestyle. You men have greatly influenced my life for the better: Dan Allender, Bob Buford, Larry Crabb, John Eldredge, Brennan Manning, Donald Miller, and Richard Rohr.

Prologue

... courage struggling for oxygen.

—Norman Maclean,
Young Men and Fire

I could begin this book by re-creating an epic scene from HBO's *Band of Brothers* or *Gladiator* or *The Lord of the Rings*. I could try to rouse your spirit by trotting out the speech William Wallace gave to those pitchfork-wielding peasants in *Braveheart*. I could pull some thread from *The Matrix* in hopes of causing you to choose the right pill and see how deep the rabbit hole goes. I could do all that and more in the opening pages of this book, but I respect you too much to do so. There is a time and place for those climactic, soul-stirring, swashbuckling moments, but this has to begin in a place we know all too well. We have to start where we are.

You probably remember the two brothers from Frank Capra's classic movie *It's a Wonderful Life*—Harry and George Bailey. In a very real sense these characters represent the two tracks of a man's life. Young Harry Bailey went off to war and returned to a hero's welcome, winning the Congressional Medal of Honor and the admiration of everyone in town. His big brother, George, however, stayed and fought the battle of Bedford Falls. No mortar fire or foxholes or clearly defined enemies for George, just day after day of the same old Bailey Building and Loan, the same drafty old house, the same wife and kids, the same Uncle Billy, the same Mr. Potter. Then came that desperate moment on the town's bridge, that end-of-the-rope belief that he was worth more dead than alive. Even the angels talked about it.

Clarence: You sent for me, sir?
Franklin: Yes, Clarence. A man down on earth needs our help.
Clarence: Splendid. Is he sick?
Franklin: No, worse. He's discouraged.

Bingo. There it is—a man with no hope. I believe that moment captures the reality of most men today—all alone, exhausted, weary, bone-tired, questioning our worth, feeling much more dead than alive, courage struggling for oxygen.

All right. While that may be the reality, I believe it's unacceptable. I don't want that for you or for me. And I don't believe one bit God desires that for the noble ones he created known as *men*. None of us began with the intention to lose heart. If you recall, George Bailey was going to travel the world. His three favorite sounds were anchor chains, plane motors, and train whistles. At one point in the black and white classic he tells young Mary Hatch:

I'm shakin' the dust of this crummy little town off my feet and I'm gonna see the world. Italy, Greece, the Parthenon, the Coliseum. Then, I'm comin' back here to go to college and see what they know. And then I'm gonna build things. I'm gonna build airfields, I'm gonna build skyscrapers a hundred stories high, I'm gonna build bridges a mile long.

But that never happened for George, or for many of us. Expectations, circumstances, family responsibilities, unexpected crises, sinful choices, and sometimes just the cards we're dealt stood in the way of our hopes to go and see and build. And after the hopes are deferred time after time after time, the heart becomes sick and discouraged, lost. You hear that train whistle blow from a distance and it just about breaks your heart.

Clarence the Angel gave George Bailey the gift of being able to see what life would be like without him. I can't give you that particular gift. But what I can share with you leads to the same truth, that each man's life touches so many others and if you're not around, it leaves an awful hole. Here's the bottom line—your life matters to this world and the people in it, and it matters to God. He has a design for your life that no one else was created to fulfill. And while I believe that truth has applied to all men in all times, there's something about the moments in which we find ourselves right now, something vital, something stirring. I believe these are monumental days—battle lines are being drawn in the epic war of good versus evil. There is a phrase for this war, taken from one of C. S. Lewis's stories—the "Last Battle." I believe this is really going to happen, and I believe you are needed. You're not expendable or replaceable. Contrary to the famous first line of a wildly successful book—*it is about you*. Sure, it may not be all about you, but it's got to be a little bit about you, or what's the point of you? Or me? Or any of us?

You may not believe that right now. That's fine. But here's the dare—keep reading. The short chapters that follow aren't wrapped in a pretty red bow; they're stained with blood and dust and sin and grace. My prayer is that you see yourself in these pages, the *you* God created and the *you* others desperately need. I realize you're tired and worn out. Guess what? Me too. But Scripture clearly teaches that you—yes, *you*—and I are called to engage in a battle, the fight of our lives, the struggle we were created for. I know that may sound like some blowhard preacher, but I believe it's true and I'm willing to stake my life on it.

Scripture doesn't indicate that thousands upon thousands of men will turn away from the bridge and step back into life with renewed strength and vision. But it does tell of a proud, happy few, a remnant, a band of barely brave men committed to hanging in there no matter the cost. In other words, you won't be alone. If you're willing to say yes to the call, I can guarantee you a few things:

- You will live out the purpose for which you were created;
- You will have an eternity filled with no regrets;
- You will have a cloud of witnesses cheering you on, including our Lord Jesus—our brother and King.

Oh yeah, one more thing—scars. There will be scars, guaranteed. But they'll be scars that mean something, scars you will tell stories about.

Note: Scattered throughout this book are links to additional material and videos of Christian brothers telling more about their stories than what you will read here. We invite you to see and experience God's heart through the lens of these sacred stories. All the video stories and additional materials for you, your small group, or church can be found at www .nomatterthecost.com. You'll also find online groups with whom you can engage in the discussions and questions from the study guide in the back of this book.

THE BEGINNING—

IT'S ABOUT YOU

For God so loved the world that he gave his one
and only son.

—John 3:16

1

What If?

We must be willing to get rid of the life we planned
so as to have the life waiting for us.

—Joseph Campbell

Do you remember those stories of the NYC firemen running up smoke-filled stairs on September 11, 2001, into the very face of hell itself? Those men risked their lives so that others might live. I believe every man wants to be a part of such a noble story—a larger story, one worth dying for and living for, where fear takes a backseat and courage takes the wheel. Undoubtedly those 9/11 heroes experienced great fear in the face of such adversity, but they weren't paralyzed by it; their greater desire to rescue others gave them the courage to be overcomers, heroes.

But what do we do on days when towers aren't falling or the nation isn't under siege? What do we do on days when we're faced with the same old family and job and church and commute and life? That's where we need a story that's grand enough to encompass both days: the called-for-heroics of a September 11 and the same-old-same-old of a September 10. I believe a story that big is only found in one place—the Bible, God's Word. All other stories, as tempting as they may be, are too small; they cannot bring you a life of strength and honor or keep you truly alive.

> anyone or anything
> that does not bring you alive
> is too small for you.
> —David Whyte,
> "Sweet Darkness"

Scripture teaches that Satan has literally *declared war* on all who proclaim to follow Jesus (Revelation 12:17). Please don't miss this—if you claim to be a Christ-follower, you and your family are under constant ruthless and brutal attacks from supreme evil. Satan is described as "wild and raging with anger; he hasn't much time and he knows it" (Revelation 12:12 THE MESSAGE). After the fall of Adam and Eve God says to the serpent, "I'm declaring war between you and the Woman, between your offspring and hers" (Genesis 3:15 THE MESSAGE).

So this much we know—the backdrop for the Last Battle is not a placid lake or some sun-kissed meadow, but a battlefield. Sorry, but that's the deal. So, as you can see, every day is somewhat like September 11 even though it may not feel like it. Since that horrible September day we have been in a war against terrorists who like to remain hidden and unseen. The spiritual war we are facing is similar, against "evil rulers and authorities of the unseen world" (Ephesians 6:12 NLT).

Scripture also reveals the final battle plan of how evil will ultimately be defeated in the Last Battle, the war to end all wars; it is strategically placed in the Bible's most prophetic book:

> They defeated [the accuser] through the blood
> of the Lamb
> and the bold word of their witness.
> They weren't in love with themselves;
> they were willing to die for Christ.
> —Revelation 12:11 THE MESSAGE

Scripture indicates Satan *will be* conquered and peace *will be* restored by those described by the word *they*—warriors some Bible versions call "the saints." Some have identified these saints as the true disciples of Christ described throughout the New Testament. These pieces of the Last Battle present a soul-searching question to us, one that I hope you'll answer as you read this book:

"Will you be one of the saints used by God to finally defeat evil?"

This is not about running around Chicken Little–style because the sky is falling. This is about banding together and bucking up because the King is coming, and possibly coming soon if the men of God will stop colluding with the evil one and instead stand and rise up, literally for Christ's sake. Make no mistake, our God has the power to defeat evil merely by willing it to be done. As he spoke the universe into existence with a word, he could extinguish evil with a breath. But Scripture teaches that he has chosen to use his saints in this conquest. Again, Scripture asks:

"Will you be one of the saints used by God to finally defeat evil?"

Will you be one of the broken men who has embraced the forgiveness offered through Christ's blood? Will you be one of God's sons willing to boldly share your testimony, your story, all of it? Will you stand as one of the faithful few willing to follow Christ—no matter the cost—even if it means losing your very life in the process? And can you see that God's fight for purity, holiness, and righteousness will not be accomplished by a singular you, but only when you are a part of the plural "they"—the saints?

I won't be vague about this. I believe we are living in the final moments, the concluding scenes in a long battle between good and evil. Notice I did not say "last days," as I believe those began when Christ ascended back to heaven. No, these are the final moments, when God is rallying his uniquely chosen army of men. Something important is happening. Something big is up.

It's often hard to put into words, but we see small bands of men rising up for the cause of Christ like never before, all around the world. Something is afoot. Don't get me wrong—I understand that many past generations felt the same way. I am not predicting dates for Christ's return, quitting my job, packing my bags, and heading for the mountains to wait for Christ to appear from the clouds. Scripture is clear on that one—only the Father knows the time and hour. Our stance is to be ready. We are commanded to be on guard and alert and to keep watch for Christ's return (Mark 13:33, 37). Needless to say, I am keenly aware that any given day may be *my* last. So regardless of when "Thy Kingdom comes," Scripture compels us to live as if Christ will return this day, or during this night, or possibly in the next breath. But what if, just what if the end or the culmination of these final moments might come sooner if men would band together, rise up, and fight shoulder to shoulder for the noble cause of Christ? What if God were waiting on us to live out this prophetic ending? What if the faithfulness of men could hasten the promise of God? What if this were true? And what if you are being called to embrace your crucial role in the Last Battle that will be talked about throughout eternity?

Luke 14 sets the conditions for what is required to be part of this story. It is a reckoning. We know that salvation is free—John 3:16 makes that clear. But our King is looking to and fro throughout the world for men who are willing to do more, the few who are willing to take the narrow road and embrace a daily bloody fight—a daily cross. Jesus tells us to not sign on the dotted line for this Last Battle until we "count the cost." Christ describes a war where there will be no terms of peace, no treaties, and no retreats. We are given a vision of the overwhelming odds we inevitably will face:

> "If you do not carry your own cross and follow me, you cannot be my disciple.
> *But don't begin until you count the cost. . . .*
> What king would go to war against another king without first sitting down with his counselors to discuss whether his army of 10,000 could defeat the 20,000 soldiers marching against him? And if he can't, he will send a delegation to discuss terms of peace while the enemy is still far away. So you cannot become my disciple without giving up everything."
>
> —Luke 14:27–28, 31–33 NLT (emphasis mine)

To be such a victorious saint demands a willingness to give up everything. Would you, could you, be a saint? Is final victory and peace worth everything you have and own—even your very life?

Our King's call to arms is very clear and concise—*Come follow me, no matter the cost.*

2

Don't Go It Alone

Don't even think about going into battle alone.
—John Eldredge, *Wild at Heart*

A Brother's Story

November—

I told her last night, told her everything. Confession is good for the soul? That phrase feels like boulders on my chest right now because the heaviness is such that I can hardly breathe. I have never ached like this, ever. Until now. She asked me to leave for now, leave the children, her, the house, everything. God, I'm so afraid. I'm so sorry. I can't even begin to know the depths of what she's feeling—betrayal, abandonment, shame, anger, devastation. How can I ever be forgiven? How could I have been so deceitful? How can I ever look into her eyes again? And what about the eyes of my children? I smell like death. Lord, you gave me so many opportunities to run. Friends warned me, but I was a blind fool. I am a sheep that was led to the slaughter. I thought that pornography viewed in my secret life wouldn't hurt anyone, but I continued to spiral and spiral into greater levels of darkness. How did my life become so dark, so evil? Who have I become? Is there any hope? It is so hard to breathe. She let me stop by the house today to pick up some clothes. She turned over our wedding pictures, all of them, monuments of broken vows. I broke them. Maybe this is beyond for better or worse. I'd swear I hear Satan's laughter. God, help. . . .

—Vance Brown

www.nomatterthecost.com/Vance-Brown

I wrote those words seventeen years ago. Typing them again brings tears to my eyes saddled to a shortness of breath. You may have a similar story. Maybe you didn't have a physical affair, but can you relate to living in such darkness? I'm willing to bet you can. Those were some of my George Bailey moments, when I felt the best thing to do for everyone involved, including myself, was to limp off the stage of my life's story, somehow draw the curtain and fade to black—*the end*. Even after all these years I still wonder how I fell so far. I was, as they say, living the dream. I had a beautiful wife and kids. My roles as both lawyer and software entrepreneur had bestowed worldly success and its trappings. I was an elder in the church I loved. Yet something wasn't working. Somehow, somewhere along the way, I got lost. As Don Henley sings, "Men get lost sometimes as years unfurl."

Then one morning everything about my life looked different. I had been consistently yielding to Satan's temptations, so God allowed me to be handed over to the evil one (see 1 Corinthians 5:5). It was like the cloak of protection was removed and hell's fury engulfed me. The next thing I knew I was sleeping at a friend's home. I had been fired from my job. About the only thing I felt my church offered in the moment was shame. That wasn't entirely true, but in my state of mind all I could hear were lies. I was suffering from severe anxiety and depression. I really couldn't see any reason to live. I knew exactly how George Bailey felt—yeah, worth more dead than alive. I was empty, done, spent, broke. Here's the first half of a poem titled "Broke":

> He woke up broken.
> Not Humpty-Dumpty broken,
> more like *broke.*
> Not ain't-got-no-money broke
> (although that's true),
> but mainly, you know, *broke*—
> not worth fixing.

I share those words with you because the spirit throughout this book must be honest. I want to tell the truth. They are not words to shock you or validate myself or to try to be authentic, as is fashionable these days. Those words are a part of my story, a part of me that I will unpack more in this book. I'd love to tell you that God redeemed those words in a *wonderful life* finale, with people coming out of the woodwork when they found I was in trouble, and bells ringing on Christmas tree branches and in church belfries, and all being right in a black-and-white world. I wish that were the case. But that didn't happen. Here's the second half of the poem "Broke":

> He prayed for an invasion of angels
> to come and heal him
> of this grievous wound,
> but God decided instead
> to send him friends,
> men who also knew *broke.*

What did happen in my life was *good,* as in "confession is good for the soul" good. God mercifully placed in my life a handful of men who could see something I could not—my worth, my reason for living. I was blinded by pain, too badly wounded, too bloody, too ashamed. One of them, a special man named Brent, heard my confession and asked through the eyes of grace, "Really, Vance? Is that it?" I couldn't believe my ears. Trust me, he was in no way diminishing what I'd done; people were hurt, people I dearly loved. But what Brent wanted to ensure was that *I* was not diminished, the "I" Christ came to seek and save, the "me" God knit together so many years ago in my mother's womb. Brent fought to show me the larger story and rescued me from the grave, as did Pete and Matt and other men. Without them my story might have ended before its time. Without the dogged belief of other men in me, I might not have stood once more by my wife, Betsy, and our three children, restored, forgiven, able to breathe again. Without a Band of Brothers by my side, I might not have been around to walk beside my son Collin, who has bravely battled the dragon named cancer. These valiant broken men said, "Your story is not going to end like this, Vance. Your family needs you. We need you. And God wants to use you. One of these days it'll end, but not yet."

Over ten years ago John Eldredge wrote these words: "Most messages for men ultimately fail. The reason is simple: They ignore what is deep and true to a man's heart." What followed was a wave of men, and the women who love them, reading a book titled *Wild at Heart.* I, thankfully, was one of those men. Tucked near the end of chapter 9 was this warning: "Don't even think about going into battle alone." But many of the men I know missed those crucial words; they've spent the last decade soldiering on, solo.

In God's great battle stories, men do not fight alone: Jonathan had David, Moses had Aaron, and Paul never traveled without a companion. And "the Lord now chose . . . other disciples and sent them ahead in pairs" (Luke 10:1 NLT). In the Last Battle there will be no "Lone Rangers." (Even the Lone Ranger in that old American western needed his Indian friend Tonto!) Jesus modeled brotherhood by surrounding himself with twelve other men. The final prayer of Jesus was that his disciples would become one, just as he and the Father are one. One thing is certain: We cannot defeat the Enemy on our own.

The greatest lesson I've learned since my George Bailey moments seventeen years ago is that I would never live out what I was created for without my brother Brent, my brother Pete, and the other men who have believed in me. Men need more than a vision or inspiration to accomplish something great; we need other men; we need comrades beside us in battle. As Eldredge wrote, "Don't even think about going into battle alone."

Here's that poem intact:

> He woke up broken.
> Not Humpty-Dumpty broken,
> more like *broke*.
> Not ain't-got-no-money broke
> (although that's true),
> but mainly, you know, *broke*—
> not worth fixing.
> He prayed for an invasion of angels
> to come and heal him
> of this grievous wound,
> but God decided instead
> to send him friends,
> men who also knew *broke*.
>
> —J. B.

3

You're So Close

They defeated [the accuser] through the blood
of the Lamb and the bold word of their witness.
They weren't in love with themselves; they were
willing to die for Christ.

—Revelation 12:11 THE MESSAGE

The prophetic verse of Revelation 12:11 is much like
standing at the lip of the Grand Canyon. It gives us the
big-picture, panoramic view for overcoming evil and finding
final peace, a promise to certainly take your breath away. But
to fully experience the grandeur of the canyon you need a trail
map, something closer to the ground to lead you across Surprise Valley, for example, and down to the deafening thunder
of Deer Creek Falls. I believe a similar kind of map is needed
to help us navigate the overarching truth of Revelation 12:11.
Chances are good you're somewhat familiar with it.

It happened that while Jesus was praying in a certain place, after He had finished, one of His disciples said to Him, "Lord, teach us to pray."

—Luke 11:1 NASB

I'm willing to roll the dice and say you've always considered the Lord's Prayer as just that—a prayer. I mean, after all, the disciples did ask Jesus to "teach us to *pray*." But I'd also wager that you often view prayer as something done in a quiet place, possibly with head bowed and eyes closed, maybe even something you're uncomfortable doing, especially in public. Is that fair? So the Lord's Prayer probably doesn't rank high on the list of inspiring scriptural passages for many men. But what if those words were intended to be so much more than a prayer? What if they are the CliffsNotes to the greatest story ever told—words that tell us not only about God, but about ourselves? What if it's a twelve-line topographic of the Last Battle?

You can look at the disciples' request to Jesus in a very one-dimensional way; they wanted to know what words to say and Jesus told them. Period, end of discussion. But Scripture repeatedly presents Jesus as anything but one-dimensional. What if, when the disciples asked Jesus to teach them to pray, they were asking for a story line to follow, a trail map for how to face battles ahead like he would? What if, on a deeper level, they were asking him to teach them how to live? And what if Jesus essentially said, *All right, this is what following me looks like; this is what becoming a part of my Last Battle is all about.* If that's the case, and I believe it is, then Jesus' words are an invitation to live, a call to arms, a bracing cost of discipleship, a ground-level map to hold on to for dear life. I believe it encapsulates the terror and the beauty

37

of the Christian life. If you want to know what a saint is, it's someone who lives these lines, the Lord's story line, the only story big enough for you and me.

> Our Father, who art in heaven,
> hallowed be thy name.
> Thy Kingdom come,
> thy will be done,
> on earth as it is in heaven.
> Give us this day our daily bread.
> And forgive us our trespasses,
> as we forgive those who trespass against us.
> And lead us not into temptation,
> but deliver us from evil.
> For thine is the kingdom, the power, and the glory,
> forever and ever.
> Amen.

I have to tell you this is a dangerous moment in the book. Because right now you're possibly thinking that just because you're familiar with the Lord's Prayer, you *know* the Lord's Prayer. Because of that, you might be tempted to skim the pages that follow, gloss over them at best, or possibly put the book aside for another day. All right, here I go again—I dare you to keep reading. To stop at this point would be like standing on the north rim of the Grand Canyon, a map for the Bill Hall trail in hand, and then refusing to step over the edge.

I have a good friend who hiked the Bill Hall. He and two friends spent four days in the belly of the canyon. Man, they've got some good stories. But one he told gave me an ache in my chest. It still does when I think about it. He told of their final push out of the canyon, from the river up to the rim in one day. As they reached the top, he noticed a group of tourists standing there watching them intently. They had

not been down in the canyon. He called them the "so-close."
As he and his friends walked over to their truck, the "so-close" couldn't help but stare at their sunburned faces, dusty boots, and salt-encrusted eyebrows. The "so-close" had no intent on going over the edge; whether due to fear or lack of time or some other more than likely valid reason, they were content to stay on the rim, glance at the grandeur, and snap some photos. What those men didn't or couldn't realize is that to truly experience the Grand Canyon you have to step over the edge, follow some switchbacks where you lose your water bottles, partially blow out a knee, and awake to find a turkey buzzard in your tent. I told you they have some good stories. That ache I spoke of earlier comes from my friend telling me of the common thread in the faces of those "so-close" men—what Thoreau tagged as "quiet desperation."

You're close right now, so close. You do not want to miss out. There are stories to be told.

THE MIDDLE—

IT'S
ABOUT
US

We and the world, my children, will always be
at war.
Retreat is impossible.
Arm yourselves.

—Leif Enger, *Peace Like a River*

4

Courage for the Battle

It doesn't interest me if there is one God or many
    gods.
I want to know if you belong or feel abandoned.
                              —David Whyte, "Self Portrait"

ood poets sometimes throw you a curve in the first
line. It's often a test to see if you've got the grit to keep
reading and not be scared away so easily. That's what David
Whyte is doing. It's possible his first line offends you—"What
do you mean? Sure, there's only one God, the one true God of
Abraham, Isaac, and Jacob!" But the poet just wants to get a
rise out of you. If you stay with him, he casts out further in
the second line, into waters beyond surface tensions of "one
God or many gods."

I want to know if you belong or feel abandoned.

If I asked you that question right now, how would you
answer? There's no middle ground here; it's an either/or

question that pertains to *most* days in your life. Don't answer too quickly. Do you feel abandoned? Have you been abandoned by your friends? By people you just knew you could depend on, but when it all hit the fan, they were nowhere to be found? What about a church? Have you given your heart and soul over the years to a church only to see everything about it change to fit today's fashions? How about abandoned by a trusted colleague at work? You never dreamed he'd betray you, but he did, more than once, and it doesn't seem to bother him at all.

Maybe you feel abandoned by life itself, or more specifically, abandoned by God. You used to have a certainty about God—not like you understood everything, but you could trust him. But now all those certainties have faded. Maybe God's got more important things to do or more important men to listen to, or maybe you've crossed the center line one too many times, or who knows. You just know it feels like you're on your own, abandoned. Sorta like Gideon.

> Whenever the Israelites planted their crops, the Midianites, Amalekites and other eastern peoples invaded the country. They camped on the land and ruined the crops all the way to Gaza and did not spare a living thing for Israel, neither sheep nor cattle nor donkeys. They came up with their livestock and their tents like swarms of locusts. It was impossible to count them or their camels; they invaded the land to ravage it. Midian so impoverished the Israelites that they cried out to the Lord for help.
>
> When the Israelites cried out to the Lord because of Midian, he sent them a prophet, who said, "This is what the Lord, the God of Israel, says: I brought you up out of Egypt, out of the land of slavery. I rescued you from the hand of the Egyptians. And I delivered you from the hand of all your oppressors; I drove them out before you and gave you their

land. I said to you, 'I am the Lord your God; do not worship the gods of the Amorites, in whose land you live.' But you have not listened to me."

The angel of the Lord came and sat down under the oak in Ophrah that belonged to Joash the Abiezrite, where his son Gideon was threshing wheat in a winepress to keep it from the Midianites. When the angel of the Lord appeared to Gideon, he said, "The Lord is with you, mighty warrior."

"Pardon me, my lord," Gideon replied, "but if the Lord is with us, why has all this happened to us? Where are all his wonders that our ancestors told us about when they said, 'Did not the Lord bring us up out of Egypt?' But now the Lord has *abandoned* us and given us into the hand of Midian."

—Judges 6:3–13 (emphasis mine)

The outside forces were too much. They ravaged the land and left the people impoverished. The situation was desperate, a definite low point. The Abiezrites were the highest-ranking family in the tribe of Manasseh. But in the midst of this destruction, one of their treasured sons was doing the work of a servant. Gideon was found threshing wheat. Let me try to paraphrase from that point.

The angel of the Lord shows up out of nowhere and takes a break under an oak tree. Gideon just happens to be close-by. The angel says, "The Lord is with you, mighty warrior." Gideon wipes his forehead with the rag from his back pocket, looks across the horizon, and says, "Look, chief. I'm sorry, but you gotta be kidding me. Sure, once it was pretty good, amazing even. But not anymore. If he's with us, why has all this happened? He's abandoned us."

Why has all this happened to us? It's an older man's question. A young man wrestles with "Why is there evil and suffering in the world?" He may even seek to build his life around alleviating it. But the older you get, the more personal it becomes: Why is there evil and suffering in *my* life? Why has this happened to *my* family, *my* kids, *my* business, *my* church—*us*? As an older man, let me give you my answer. Life is a battle. We are at war, but it's different than you think. I want to tell you two war stories. They're both true.

War Story #1

We both love the same woman. Her name is Betsy; she's his daughter and my wife. His name is Paul Johanon, one of the bravest men I know. I'll never forget the Thanksgiving meal where he shared a little of his World War II experiences. I knew he rarely voiced his war stories, but on that particular holiday, around the table in his own home, my wife's first hero graciously opened his memories.

December 7, 1941, and the attack on Pearl Harbor was to change many lives, and certainly my own. It was the beginning of a new life for me. I could no longer do my own thing. I had surrendered to the U.S. Army, and now I belonged to them. The training I had to bear before being sent into battle was intense. I had to do the drills over and over. But hindsight tells me it was for my good. I had to clear out the enemy mines so General Patton's tanks could arrive. . . . I'll never forget our amphibious landing in Sicily. It was the largest operation prior to the Normandy invasion. Mines on the beach and machine-gun fire made our advancement very difficult and costly. . . . On one occasion during an intense battle we saw several men in a field wounded after an explosion. The field was covered in land mines. A couple of us grabbed a medic and set out to tend and rescue those wounded men. I would disarm the mines and open a path so the medic could reach the men. We were able to save some of those men.

"But why did you risk your life when you didn't have to?" I asked. "You could have just played it safe, staying out of harm's way. Was it worth it?"

When a buddy was wounded, you didn't even think about it—you just did it. Yes, it was worth it all. We were fighting for the liberation of the free world. We were there to stop a crazed killer named Hitler; he was killing innocent men and women.

I was spellbound. As I sat listening to my father-in-law, the smile on the face of his wife of fifty years was impossible to miss. It was that wordless gesture of the long-married that said, "That's my man!" I have to admit that the look she gave him unsettled me. You see, I had worked hard in the business world. I practiced law for a season, started a successful software company, and later became CEO of Goldmine Software Corporation. Most, if not all, of my boxes were checked:

☑ pretty wife?
☑ cute kids?
☑ good job?
☑ nice house?
☑ active in local church?

But I didn't know if all those accolades would have gotten me a "That's my man!" smile from my wife. Something wasn't adding up. My father-in-law had been awarded a Purple Heart for his heroic efforts. The only heart I had was sick, tired, exhausted, worn out. Mr. Johanon had fought for a noble cause. I had been fighting just because. I battled hard at work, but it wasn't something I would die for. My job was important by today's standards, but my story felt fragile when measured against "fighting a crazed killer." I was living the good life, but not living a good life. I felt like I'd been born in the wrong generation. Have you ever felt like that? No crazed killers on the horizon, just unread emails. No sweeping hordes of evil to stand against, no mines to disarm or tanks to accompany, nothing anywhere close to that kind of a cause.

> . . . an entire generation pumping gas, waiting tables; slaves with white collars. Advertising has us chasing cars and clothes, working jobs we hate so we can buy [stuff] we don't need. We're the middle children of history, man. No purpose or place. We have no Great War. No Great Depression. Our Great War's a spiritual war . . . our Great Depression is our lives. We've all been raised on television to believe that one day we'd all be millionaires, and movie gods, and rock stars. But we won't. And we're slowly learning that fact.
>
> —Tyler Durden, *Fight Club*

War Story #2

Years ago my life intersected with a man who began a journey with me through the futility and anxiety in my life. His name was Brent Curtis, coauthor of *The Sacred Romance* with John Eldredge. I went to see Brent because I was beaten and battered—"courage struggling for oxygen," as Norman Maclean puts it. At the conclusion of our very first meeting, Brent gave me a visual I'll never forget: "Picture yourself at the bottom of a rock canyon—bleeding and broken—and you can't get up. I promise you, one day you will get up and walk out of that rock canyon."

May 1998. Brent and John had invited me to join them for a retreat in the mountains of Colorado. As we all gathered the second night, Brent began sharing about "the wildness of God" as if it was a good thing. I remember protesting: "I don't like the wildness of God! At times I don't feel like I can take it anymore!"

"But he is good," Brent responded. I admit my skepticism. This was years before C. S. Lewis's *Narnia* quote—"He's not safe, but he's good"—came into vogue.

The third day held an afternoon of rock-climbing. Brent asked me to accompany him early to get things set up. I drove with him to a nearby rock canyon, and then we walked together into the valley. The sun was brilliant and the sky was a color of blue you find only in Colorado; it was a perfect day. As we approached the site, Brent pointed to a rock formation at the top of the canyon. He explained his plan of tying off a rope around the rock and then dropping the rope to me. The next thing I knew, Brent was seated on the rock, tying the rope around it, and then he slipped and fell. He tumbled down some eighty feet of rock cliff, finally landing exactly where I'd been standing only seconds before. Moments earlier we'd been talking and laughing like friends do. And just like that my friend was gone.

I said good-bye to him at the bottom of that canyon. I just about said good-bye to God as well; it felt like the last straw. Is this what following "the wild God" involved? Surely this wasn't God's will. Why? What? Brent Curtis left a wife and two small boys, and a cadre of men. I walked out of that rock canyon, bloodied and broken in my own way, and remembered Brent's prophetic words to me. I suddenly found myself painfully aware of a reality I'd only begun to sense; I couldn't necessarily see it, but I could feel it.

—Vance Brown

As I said, both of these war stories are true. A fool believes it's one or the other, either the battle you can see with actual tanks or emails or the unseen spiritual battle that shows itself occasionally, and then only in glimpses. I don't want to be a fool, and I don't want you to be one either. It's both. I believe the wise man lives in that tension. There are two battles. The struggle may not be against flesh and blood, but it sure feels that way, doesn't it? To admit that means you're alive and actually living on the earth instead of existing in some otherworldly place, what some refer to as being "so heavenly minded you're no earthly good." Yeah, that doesn't help anyone. But living with an awareness that there's something behind the flesh and blood, something you can't always see but something you can feel? That's the kind of tension I'm talking about, that there's the lowercase and the uppercase—the battle and the Battle. Author Frederick Buechner describes it this way:

> We fight to be visible, to move into a place in the sun, a place in the family, the community, in whatever profession we choose, a place where we can belong, where there is light enough to be recognized as a person and to keep the shadows at bay. . . . It is the war of flesh against flesh: to get ahead, to win, to gain or regain power, to survive in a world where not even survival is had without struggle. . . . But there is another war that we fight.
>
> —"The Two Battles"

> For our struggle is not against flesh and blood, but against the rulers, against the authorities, against the powers of this dark world and against the spiritual forces of evil in the heavenly realms.
>
> —Ephesians 6:12

Let's go back to Gideon's question: *Why has all this happened to us?* Life is a battle. We are being ruthlessly and brutally attacked. Sure, some have taken that metaphor and strained it for their own purposes. That's not what I'm talking about. I'm trying to be a witness to what I sense, what I believe you sense as well, and what Scripture teaches: Something is wrong with the world. If you're in a battle, you're going to get hurt. You're going to face challenges and setbacks. To go through life without so much as a scratch is impossible; even fairy tales have dragons. The temptation, especially when the battle seems fierce and the odds are overwhelming, is to conclude that God has abandoned you. The truth is that just like in Gideon's story, God is right there. "The Lord answered, 'I will be with you'" (Judges 6:16).

But it takes something to see him.

During the most difficult season of my life, I heard God say the following:

> The Last Battle is beginning, and its intensity is escalating. Evil is advancing against the forces of good. I am asking you and others to engage in this war. The stories that unfold will echo throughout eternity. The battle will be fierce. I am the Good God, and the rewards for fighting and finishing with me are more than you can imagine. You will feel alone at times, but know that I am your God and I am with you. Your unique skills and gifts are vital to this battle, but only if they are used alongside the skills and gifts of other brothers. I want you to be brave and proud. Be righteous. Take courage.

I'd bet I know what some of you are thinking right now: "Now, there's the ultimate trump card. . . . God told you! Yeah, right! So how do you *know* God told you this? Couldn't that feeling of a 'word from God' simply have been something you ate from the night before?" My answer: I cannot prove this to anyone, nor do I believe that is my responsibility. I can only believe what I believe and be a witness to what I believe, as long as it is consistent with Scripture. And I believe it to be true with all my heart. Even as a child, I had recurring dreams about the end moments and Christ's return. Accordingly, I want to live my life as if it is true. I don't want to miss out. You, however, need to discern for yourself the truth of this message. But in our Band of Brothers ministry we are hearing the essence of this message echoed around the world. God is rallying together his army, Christ's true followers.

By the way, did you catch that last word in what God spoke to me? *Courage.* "But the Lord said to him, 'Peace! Do not be afraid'" (Judges 6:23).

Courage. That's what Gideon needed. It's what we need too.

I can already hear you. Courage, schmourage. You've heard calls for courage before, right? Me too. It gets exhausting, doesn't it, always trying to rouse your courage to meet whatever challenge is ahead? I get it. But what if I told you I believe we've been slightly misled? That the rousing stuff is part of it, no doubt, but maybe not where it begins. I say that because of where the word *courage* comes from, its roots. Our word originates from the French *coeur,* meaning "heart." I know, I know, stay with me a moment.

Do you know what the antidote for exhaustion is? Probably nine out of every ten of us would respond with one word—*rest.* But I've come to see that's part of our problem. The antidote to exhaustion is not necessarily rest, but wholeheartedness. Think about that a moment. When are you exhausted? I'm not talking about being tired, like after a good workout or mowing the grass, but exhausted, spent, weary? For me it's when I've got too many irons in the fire, too many plates spinning in midair, too many windows open on my browser. I'm not singularly focused or committed to one thing but am being pulled in a number of different directions, trying to give my allegiance to everything out there.

What if courage for the battle comes from seeking one thing above all others and letting everything else follow from there? What if the heart you and I have lost could be found in the pursuit of a single goal? What if that feeling of being abandoned has its origins in trying to gain the world while knowing deep within you're losing your soul?

Wholeheartedness. No matter the cost. That's where courage comes from. That's where belonging comes from. But just what is this one thing? Miss this point and you'll spend the second half of your life repeating the mistakes of the first. You'll waste your pain instead of learning from it. You've given your allegiance to the church, the workplace, your family, your marriage, your kids, your body, and the list goes on. All of them necessary, and all lead to exhaustion. But there is one that rises above "necessary" . . . one that is noble, one that we must seek first.

The original warrior-poet put it this way:

> But seek first the kingdom of God and his righteousness, and all these things will be added to you.
>
> —Matthew 6:33 ESV

We are being called into the Last Battle and we need courage to engage. True courage comes from wholeheartedness, seeking first . . . *our Father, who art in heaven.*

5

The F-Word

Our *Father,* who art in heaven . . .

A Brother's Story

My house was like a war zone—screaming, yelling, and my making calls to the police to break up fights. Then the day came that Dad was gone. . . . I remember being on the lawn looking up at the clouds wondering if I would ever see him again. The months rolled by, but they seemed like years. He wasn't around, physically or emotionally. My parents finally divorced when I was nine; after that I'd only see my dad every two weeks. Sometimes he would pick me up for those visits and sometimes he'd have someone else come and get me. I remember wanting to be with him; it didn't matter where or what was going on, I just wanted to be with him. I don't remember him giving me any advice, like "Watch out for these things, Pete." We never had the sex talk, and the only encouragement I recall came on my junior high graduation—"Good job." Most of life I had to figure out for myself.

My mom tried to fill the void left by my dad, but she couldn't. I was acting out, a rebel without a cause, mainly a rebel without a father. I got kicked out of the house by my mother at age fourteen; there was a note attached to my bag that said, "Go live with your dad." I did.

My father served in WWII. I admired that, but any time I brought it up, he changed the conversation. After my parents divorced, my dad signed up for the sexual revolution of the '60s. He was still a member when I showed up to live with him. An atmosphere of sexual freedom is risky for a grown man; it's completely toxic for a fourteen-year-old boy. Unfortunately, I concluded women were not to be trusted and they existed merely to satisfy men.

Eventually, I became a senior in high school, but I did not have enough credits to graduate. So I quit school and joined the work world to survive, and it was a hard world. I was still alone, but now I had to figure out life for myself financially. All of this past was a great setup for the Enemy to have the ammo to fire at will. All of the questions—"Why I am here?" and "What's the point?" and "Do I have what it takes?"—continued to haunt me. I had no college education, and my life and my job felt futile and hopeless. Sex was one way to be a man, and drugs were a way to medicate the pain of the unknown.

My dad's relationship with God, if you want to call it that, was completely performance based. That weak thread eventually snapped; his lifestyle was just too hard to reconcile with anything to do with God. Due to God's grace, I became a Christian and my life started to change. I began to have some hope. Dad didn't buy it; he thought I was a fake and took the liberty more than once of dismissing the people and things I cared for. It's like he wanted to destroy everything I loved, even if that included him. Needless to say, to this very day the word *father* is difficult to understand.

—Pete Gannon

The F-word—*father*. Jesus could have chosen any word to begin his prayer: God, Lord, Master, Savior, Redeemer, Creator. But he didn't. Sometimes I wish he had; it would have made things a little bit easier, because those six letters haunt most of us on some level every day of our lives. Imagine a roomful of men having a conversation about their fathers; the room would be combustible, and that's probably an understatement. That word—*father*—is broken and splintered by the sin and shame in our world. But that's the word Jesus chose. It helps to remember that Jesus was very clear that he didn't come for the healthy; instead, he came for the sick and the broken. He came to restore and redeem those held captive.

> Jesus answered them, "It is not the healthy who need a doctor, but the sick."
>
> —Luke 5:31

> "The Spirit of the Lord is on me, because he has anointed me to proclaim good news to the poor. He has sent me to proclaim freedom for the prisoners and recovery of sight for the blind, to set the oppressed free."
>
> —Luke 4:18

I believe this even applies to words, words that are realities, words like *father*.

Now, in all fairness, maybe your father did well by you, and your life is a poor attempt to imitate him. Maybe your father was like Solomon Vandy in the film *Blood Diamond*. Solomon loved his son more than his own life. Solomon's son, Dia, was taken by rebels and forced into a boy-soldier lifestyle, commanded to witness and commit unspeakable sins. In the parable of the prodigal son, the father waits for his youngest to return. In a twist on that familiar story, this father travels to find his prodigal. Solomon navigates harm's way and finally finds Dia, only to be held at gunpoint by the son who has almost forgotten what it's like to be a son.

> Dia, what are you doing? Dia! Look at me, look at me. What are you doing? You are Dia Vandy, of the proud Mende tribe. You are a good boy who loves soccer and school. Your mother loves you so much. She waits by the fire making plantains, and red palm oil stew with your sister N'Yanda and the new baby. The cows wait for you. And Babu, the wild dog who minds no one but you. I know they made you do bad things, but you are not a bad boy. I am your father who loves you. And you will come home with me and be my son again.

It's impossible for me to watch that scene and not be moved, most of the time to tears.

Press the pause button just a minute, because I want to point to something early on here—the sacredness of tears. My editor described this book as a text for "the postmodern men's movement." I'm not sure if I know what all that means. When I think about the word *post* I usually think post-9/11. Everything is different now after that black September day; we're all a little further east of the garden:

> I do not remember any of their far-away names,
> those raptured into spacious skies that day.
> But I do remember her,
> as I remember me, cast ready-or-not
> further east of the garden.
> —J. B.

That day changed our nation and it changed our world. Everything now is after that day—"post." This book is for men who've had their own 9/11 experience, that day when the towers fell down. Maybe it was the tower of marriage or job or family or friendship or good health or some combination of all of them. Whatever it was, it collapsed in a heap of rubble and smoke. If you've had that experience, you know about tears; you're a misty-eyed man.

> And yes not only boys but men can cry. And men not only can cry but there are times when, in their humanity, they should cry.
>
> —Robert Olen Butler

Those tears don't indicate weakness and they're nowhere near crocodile tears. No, they're signs of brokenness, and I believe they are sacred. Trust me, this doesn't mean we sit around in some weep-fest passing Kleenex to each other; that's not what I mean. I mean if you're paying attention, you'll see a tear drop from the corner of my eye from time to time. I try not to wipe them away but just let them drop. Why? It's because of a promise in the Bible's last book:

> "He will wipe every tear from their eyes. There will be no more death" or mourning or crying or pain, for the old order of things has passed away.
>
> —Revelation 21:4

One of these days God will wipe away the tears from the war-weary faces of his saints. Until then, let them fall where and when they may.

All right, thanks for that moment. Now back to *father*. When I watch that scene from *Blood Diamond*, it brings tears to my eyes; tears are telling me something. I believe they're telling me about the brokenness between my father and me. Frederick Buechner calls them "homesick tears"—that feeling that things weren't as we hoped they would be. There never was a scene like that in my childhood; I don't remember hearing "I love you" in my early years. The love I felt came mostly from my performance and accomplishments rather than from my identity in Christ. So those tears come from a longing I had and still have. The relationship between my father and me was okay; not great, just okay. I don't remember many deep conversations back then. We bonded mainly around the common ground of sports, and growing up in Durham, North Carolina, that meant one thing—Duke. I've come to that point where I don't blame my dad, and we've since learned to better show and express our love for one another. But that doesn't mean the longing goes away. I still want more. I'm still homesick.

Then again, maybe your father was a violent man who made your life a living hell and as soon as you could get away you did. Two of the men in my Band of Brothers grew up with abusive, alcoholic fathers. Maybe your father was like that, some combustible mix of the Godfather and the Great Santini; there may have been a veneer of love, but you sure didn't turn your back on him. Or maybe he was like another brother's father, a good Christian man who worked six days a week, was usually there for dinner, and led regular family devotions; physically present but emotionally absent. Or maybe your father was literally absent; you don't know quite what you feel about the word *father* because he wasn't around, sorta like Pete's dad. But you do know an ache, the one that comes out as a long and profound sighing of the heart.

I wonder what those first disciples thought when Jesus pulled that word out of the bag. Of the men who first answered the call of "Follow me," we know next to nothing about their lives before Jesus came along, certainly little about their fathers. James and John are noted in Scripture as the sons of Zebedee, and on one occasion Jesus names them "the sons of thunder." This phrase surely says something about these brothers, but I wonder if it doesn't also say something about Zebedee? Was he impetuous, loud, fiery, zealous, likely to be the one to cause a commotion, and his sons came by those traits naturally? We don't know for sure. What we do know is that whatever the word *father* meant to those men on that day, Jesus took that word and made it the starting point, the first step toward truly experiencing what it meant to be a saint. It's almost like some divine gauntlet that Jesus throws out and says, "He is the Father. He is where it began, where it continues, and where it will end. Whatever your experience has been with the word, he's more than that, so *much more*."

> "Which of you, if your son asks for bread, will give him a stone? Or if he asks for a fish, will give him a snake? If you, then, though you are evil, know how to give good gifts to your children, how *much more* will your Father in heaven give good gifts to those who ask him!"
>
> —Matthew 7:9–11 (emphasis mine)

A few lines ago I said I was homesick. While I wonder sometimes why Jesus began his prayer with the word *Father*, at other times I understand. *Father*—it is the word that stirs us, whether we realize or not, whether we can articulate it or not. It stirs the idea and the ideal of home. Think about William Wallace in *Braveheart* or Maximus in *Gladiator* or even Nemo, for that matter; all that struggle, all those battles, all that pain—why? To get back home. Think about the prodigal's come-to-his-senses moment: "I've got to get back to my father, back home." Jesus knew that *Father* and *home* are deep within our bones; I believe he knit them in there before

60

the very foundations of the world. They are words that hold some of our deepest pain, and because of that, they are also words that hold some of our deepest hope, the kind worth fighting for. I believe William Gibson captures the deepest hope of both fathers and sons in his novel *A Mass for the Dead*:

> The depot was seven blocks from our street, and I often met him with the car when my mother was hovering at the oven. I waited at the mouth of an underpass until he appeared in its flow of nameless men, still unique, trim and natty in his gray suit with vest, small-knotted tie, gray felt hat at a modest angle, and his face so benign and candid, alive in a smile at seeing me. . . . Now I was two inches taller than he, and surely grown much too complicated for him to understand, but my heart still like a child skipped a little at the sight of his rare figure, sauntering among the others, easily slapping with the newspaper at his calf, so contented to be home.

Pete Gannon's Story Continued

My parents did what they could in the midst of their battles, but the brutality of divorce blinded them to the carnage left in the wake of their decisions. This all may sound like I am blaming them for my issues, but I'm trying not to. This is how the stage was set for me, how my story was intended to destroy me. I had to make my own choices along the way. Many of *my* choices furthered my decline and self-worth.

Yet my desire to be restored to my father and to feel his pride in me has never ceased. Recently my dad was almost killed in a horrific car accident. He should have died. He was hospitalized for eighteen months. As it so happens, I became his caretaker, paying his bills and wiping the sweat from his brow. In the first months he couldn't even talk because of his severe injuries. In one of his speechless moments, I told my dad that I loved him. He couldn't respond with words, but I could see tears in his eyes—symbols of regret. Something broke in that moment. He couldn't talk, but he spoke volumes by holding me in his arms, for a very long time. For that brief instant in time, I was home. Not all was fixed, but there was some healing. As a man who now has lived long enough to know, I recognize those tears of regret in my own eyes for some choices I have made in life. We both have disappointments. We both want to be better men. I thank God that he gave my father and me a chance for some redemption—even if that occurred on a hospital bed.

www.nomatterthecost.com/Pete-Gannon

6

Brothers

Our Father, who art in heaven

Don't miss the brilliance of Jesus here. He qualified *Father* with the word *our*. What Jesus does for the disciples (and us) is place the prayer in the context of family and kin and immediately levels the ground. It's not that we're the same, but equal. There are those all-star verses in the Bible that get most, if not all, the attention. I'm thinking of John 3:16 or Philippians 4:13. Sometimes the verses immediately following the all-stars tend to get lost, like the one that follows the often quoted Romans 8:28:

> And we know that in all things God works for the good of those who love him, who have been called according to *his purpose*. (emphasis mine)

Do you know what the next verse says? It lays out God's "purpose" from verse 28. More than any other verse in

Scripture, I believe it captures God's very own mission statement for his children:

> For those God foreknew he also predestined to be conformed to the image of his Son, that he might be the firstborn among many *brothers*. (emphasis mine)

Did you catch that last word? *Brothers*. This completely undoes me. First Jesus pulls out the word *Father* and then has the guts to throw *brothers* in the mix. The Father is working in all things (not just some) for our good so that we can become a brother to Christ. I bet you haven't heard a sermon lately on "Being Christ's Brother." That's unfortunate, because that invitation to the royal family is a part of what the good news is all about. And it's not just about being in the family but about resembling "the firstborn"—Jesus. I can hear some of you already—"Ugh, another call to be Christlike, which usually borders on the feminine." Don't worry, this is not some call to a cookie-cutter, homogenized life; we've had enough of that.

> When the imitation of Christ does not mean to live a life like Christ, but to live your life as authentically as Christ lived his, then there are many ways and forms in which a man can be a Christian.
>
> —Henri Nouwen, *The Wounded Healer*

Many ways and forms—a phrase that grabs everyone from the warrior to the mystic to the shepherd to the prophet and the priest and shakes the cobwebs from our minds. God's invitation is to a brotherhood that doesn't strip you of your personality but redeems it for the noble cause of Christ. Most groups trying to reach men miss this:

They refuse the men themselves; they insist upon a diagram of humanity instead. They dwell only upon what they would like a man to conform to; they never come within a hundred miles of knowing what a man is.

—Robert Farrar Capon, *The Romance of the Word*

The Father "foreknew" you and chose you to be in his family, a brother to his one and only Son; his hand is upon your life throughout every trial and tribulation you go through to bring you safely home to the Father's house. But sadly, sometimes it's our own brothers we fight against most.

Jesus tells a story similar to this in Luke's gospel.

Jesus continued: "There was a man who had two sons. The younger one said to his father, 'Father, give me my share of the estate.' So he divided his property between them.

"Not long after that, the younger son got together all he had, set off for a distant country and there squandered his wealth in wild living. After he had spent everything, there was a severe famine in that whole country, and he began to be in need. So he went and hired himself out to a citizen of that country, who sent him to his fields to feed pigs. He longed to fill his stomach with the pods that the pigs were eating, but no one gave him anything.

"When he came to his senses, he said, 'How many of my father's hired servants have food to spare, and here I am starving to death! I will set out and go back to my father and say to him: Father, I have sinned against heaven and against you. I am no longer worthy to be called your son; make me like one of your hired servants.' So he got up and went to his father. . . .

"Meanwhile, the older son was in the field. When he came near the house, he heard music and dancing. So he called one of the servants and asked him what was going on. 'Your brother has come,' he replied, 'and your father has killed the fattened calf because he has him back safe and sound.'

"The older brother became angry and refused to go in. So his father went out and pleaded with him. But he answered his father, 'Look! All these years I've been slaving for you and never disobeyed your orders. Yet you never gave me even a young goat so I could celebrate with my friends. But when this son of yours who has squandered your property with prostitutes comes home, you kill the fattened calf for him!'"

—Luke 15:11–20, 25–30

Brothers. Maybe literal blood ties. Maybe you're the younger, maybe you're the older. Maybe your brother is not one by blood; he's closer than a brother. Once upon a time you were inseparable, you had big plans to work together, you dreamed dreams and had visions. But something happened along the way; it was never intended, but it happened just the same. What was it? The details are obviously different, but the word to describe it all is a variation of a story that's been repeated since time began: jealousy, rivalry, Dad-likes-you-better-than-me. Whatever you want to call it, the result is always the same. A rift or split. Division. Brokenness.

If only I had a dollar for every man I know who had a brother and then lost a brother or is severed from a brother. There was a time in my life when I hated my blood brother. My secret addictions were creeping out in ways that impacted the relationship I had with my brother. I'll never forget being called into the boardroom of the family business my brother and I led, and there sat my father, mother, and brother. And in one of those "falling tower" moments, they fired me. It's one thing to be fired by a boss or manager, but to be fired by your family, your own flesh and blood? Well, that's quite another. I left that room shell-shocked, knee-deep in shame, despising my parents and hating my brother. I wanted to kill him, I really did.

Years later I was embarking on a ministry journey with another man, a trusted friend and ally in the battle for the hearts of men and women. Everything looked so bright, so hopeful, and then in a matter of a few instances we were at odds, both of us in far countries, he in his and me in mine. Seeds of distrust had been planted that erupted in disgust and anger. Anger, as we know, is a mask for sadness and fear. I was heartbroken, stumbling around in the rubble of the aftermath feeling like someone had stolen my birthright and my blessing. I didn't know what to do, I really didn't.

I'm drawn and repelled by this "brother" piece; it excites and baffles me. Jesus decided to use *Father,* and then qualify that word with *our*—what kind of man would say something like that? As C. S. Lewis wrote in *Mere Christianity:*

> A man who was merely a man and said the sort of things Jesus said would not be a great moral teacher. He would either be a lunatic—on the level with a man who says he is a poached egg—or he would be the devil of hell. You must take your choice. Either this was, and is, the Son of God, or else a madman or something worse.

I must be candid with you. There are days I struggle with believing all I have written in this book. Sometimes it all feels just too crazy to believe. But then I remember many experiences and encounters that I cannot dismiss as "mere random coincidences." That would feel even more crazy! I call such a God-moment a *Huh?*—a time when there is no explanation other than believing what the Bible says, that there is a heavenly Father and a Jesus who is his Son. When my *Huh?* is consistent with scriptural truth, I become convinced there is a power, a larger story, a love, and a divine plan that cannot always be seen with the naked eye. Faith is required, but not a blind faith. At such times the eyes of my heart give me hope and resolve. Through my journey I have become convinced that this transcendent story is so good that I want to join in, be a part of it, and not miss out. My faith and a quiet peace are growing the more I seek to follow Jesus. So I believe Jesus was, and is, the Son of God. That is the basis of my trust, and he's saying, "Look, if you want to be a saint, you need to understand there is one God and Father of us all, and we're all brothers."

> While Jesus was still talking to the crowd, his mother and brothers stood outside, wanting to speak to him. Someone told him, "Your mother and brothers are standing outside, wanting to speak to you."
>
> He replied to him, "Who is my mother, and who are my brothers?" Pointing to his disciples, he said, "Here are my mother and my brothers. For whoever does the will of my Father in heaven is my brother and sister and mother."
>
> —Matthew 12:46–50

I want to end this chapter by mentioning something that might seem small, but I believe is anything but: the closeness of the Father. The phrase is "Our Father, who art in heaven," but just exactly where is heaven? Is it up there, out there, somewhere over the rainbow? Where do you think it is? Would you be willing to surrender all and follow a Father who was way out there somewhere, removed from the daily grind of our lives? In most of our Bible translations, the phrase "Our Father, who art in heaven" is missing something—a plural. Author Dallas Willard points out that the phrase should read "Our Father, the one in the *heavens*." If that's the case, then we're praying to a Father who is out there but is also right here. In biblical terms, "the first heaven" is as close as the breath on our face. So we can accurately pray, "Our Father, who is always near." We may feel abandoned, but as men of a certain age, we know feelings are not always trustworthy. The truth, the reality for brothers, for the saints, is that the Father is right here, always has been, always will be. He is Emmanuel—God with us!

> I will praise the Lord, who counsels me; even at night my heart instructs me. I keep my eyes always on the Lord. With him at my right hand, I will not be shaken.
>
> —Psalm 16:7–8

7

Hallowed? Really?

> I am at an impasse, and you, o God, have brought
> me here.
>
> —Nicholas Wolterstorff, *Lament for a Son*

A Brother's Story

Sometimes life feels like nothing more than days and nights. I can tell you about them; I know about them. Two days after my shoulder surgery, my life was turned upside down. I had a violent drug interaction to the pain meds and ended up in a lockdown facility sleeping next to addicts and alcoholics of every stripe. Before I go on, I must explain the ambulance ride. You see, they put me in the back of a van in a metal cage, essentially a pen reserved for drug addicts or others who had lost control. The first night out of two, my hospital roommate was a man picked up at a local bar for being too much under the influence of alcohol. He lasted only one night and then was gone. The second night was spent with a roommate who was on at least eight different pain meds and was trying to get off the high.

And me? I voluntarily checked in because my head was spinning, I hadn't slept in three days, and I truly thought I was going crazy. I really couldn't have cared less about who my roommate was, I just wanted help. My mind wouldn't shut off. It all started when I began hallucinating and had the constant sensation of falling from a twenty-story building. I told the docs that I just wanted it to stop. Nothing stopped the sensation, but it would have to stop soon, right? Nope. They tried many different medications and none of them worked. In fact, most of them made the sensation even more dramatic. To make matters worse, each time the falling effect began I would have an electrical shocking sensation in my brain. As I said before, it should go away soon, right? Nope.

And God? Well, a good God wouldn't continue to allow this, would he? Yes, he would and did. The falling and spinning and shocking lasted for months on end. And the sleep? The docs told me that surely your body will get tired out and sleep when it needs it, but that didn't happen either. I went from November 3 of one year until May 7 of the next without sleeping more than two hours per night. Do the math there; that's nuts. When I would wake up with double the dose of sleeping meds in me, I wouldn't just wake up, but jump out of bed with my heart racing and sweat pouring off my body, knowing I'd have to wait another twenty-two hours to take my next sleeping pill. The only time I felt peace was during those precious two hours of rest. What would it take to get me out of this? After months of little to no sleep I started wondering if this was somehow a punishment for all the bad things I had done. What were my wife and kids thinking? Would I ever recover? I remember those Scripture verses: "Rejoice in the Lord always. I will say it again: Rejoice!" And with *"thanksgiving,*

present your request to God, and the peace of God, which tran-
scends all understanding, will guard your heart." I prayed over
and over and over again, presenting my request to the Lord with
thanksgiving . . . but nothing happened. No peace at all, no nothing. I began to lose that precious commodity called hope. How
could a "good" God allow all of this for so long? "Hallowed" be
thy name? Really? You've got to be kidding me because I'm not
feeling it . . . and if God's not going to help me when I'm at my
lowest, then why would I praise Him when things are good? I'm
just not so sure anymore. . . .

—Pete Ohlin

A n impasse. If there were only one per lifetime then
maybe we could learn to adjust to another route or
find some way over or under or around. But there's never
just one, is there? Life is one impasse after another, and it is
in those impossible moments filled with pain and suffering
when we question the "hallowed be thy name." Pete's story
aches with the pulse of "How could a good God . . . ?" Other
stories lose the pulse; they just give up. Not long ago a lady
committed suicide not far from where I live. Sometimes it
feels like God just watches, doesn't it?

> Sometimes it's hard to understand the drift of things.
> Sources say she left a note, drove to the overpass,
> parked her pickup, paused a moment to synchronize
> with the oncoming bus below,
> then jumped.
> A forty-two-year-old sparrow fell twenty-five feet.
> God watched as traffic rerouted.
>
> —J. B.

Hallowed be thy name.

You don't hear the word *hallowed* much these days, if at all. About the only place it pops up is in mentions of Halloween. Other translations use the word *holy*, but that word may be about as hard to wrap our heads around as *hallowed*. Whether it's conscious or unconscious, I believe we put the word *good* in that line, or at least that's the word we'd choose if we could.

Our Father, who art in heaven, your name is good.

And that's where it gets hard, when things aren't good or going well. And our cry in those moments? *Rescue me, God!* When we speak those words—*rescue me, Jesus, come to my rescue*—what are we hoping for? My gut tells me we usually think about that word in a mechanistic manner, i.e., if our car stalls in the snowbank, then Jesus (a) magically starts the engine after seven tries or (b) compels Mr. Goodwrench to take a drive right by the snowbank we're stalled in and Mr. Goodwrench has just the tools to help us. That's fair, isn't it? Those are exactly the kind of *rescue* thoughts that were rolling around in the heads, hearts, minds, and souls of the people who walked in great darkness a long time ago in the pages of Scripture. We keep wanting the good Lord to show up in our name, but for some reason he insists on only showing up in his. And his name is *hallowed* or *holy*; another definition from the same family of words is *healing*.

> Perhaps . . . his help consists in his continuous presence in all victims. . . . He doesn't start your stalled car for you; he comes and dies with you in the snowbank. You can object

that he should have made a world in which cars don't stall; but you can't complain he doesn't stick by his customers.

—Robert Farrar Capon

For example, let's say Pete was struggling with anxiety for the past twelve months and I've been intentional about checking on him, for I have experienced the same torment. Today he might say, "I couldn't have made it without Vance's help," or maybe even, "Vance came to my rescue." What exactly is Pete saying? Is he talking about how I helped him think through his job and finances or that I went to the gym with him to help clear his head? Possibly. But more than likely Pete is talking about my presence in his life over the last twelve months. It's not so much what I *did*, but simply that I was *there*. I just sat in the muck with him. I stuck by the customer.

Answers to prayers for help are a problem only when you look on God as a divine vending machine programmed to dispense Cokes, Camels, lost keys, and freedom from gall-bladder trouble to anyone who has the right coins. . . . Given the kind of free world he has chosen to make—he will do the best he can by you. It isn't that he has a principle about not starting cars—or about starting them. What he has a principle about is *you*. . . . His chief concern is *to be himself for you*. . . . And since he is God, that is no small item.

—Robert Farrar Capon

Our lives and our world are broken. Our Father is about healing the brokenness of this world. There are times he does that by dramatic intervention; we use the word *miracle*. There are other times when he heals by his presence with us, and his presence is most strongly felt by the presence of another brother right there with us in the agony and confusion and tears. Having another man in the foxhole with you or in the waiting room beside you or standing shoulder to shoulder with you as they lower the casket in the ground makes all the difference between despair and hope. Healing is impossible in loneliness; in other words, it leaves us at an impasse. Healing occurs together, in companionship, in community, in brotherhood.

God is working all things together for our good, even when, and maybe most especially when, those things aren't good according to our definitions. When we pray and live "hallowed is your name," we are making an affirmation that we may get glimpses of the reasons behind the pain and suffering in this lifetime, and then again, we may not. But either way, as Robert Farrar Capon wrote, we believe God sticks by his "customers," and we commit to doing the same thing because only then can the mending and redemption and healing of our grievous wounds truly occur.

Though we walk through the valley of the shadow of death, we will fear no evil.

For thou art with us.

Pete Ohlin's Story Continued

God has restored my hope with two things: music and a Band of Brothers. Vance and other men have stuck by me in my darkest moments and I have felt the very presence of Christ. Their support and prayers have truly been healing. My wife, who was amazing through this ordeal, also found strength in the group of men who were fighting for me and my family. She didn't feel like she was going at it alone. I still don't understand everything that happened to me; maybe I never will. My pastor, Andy Stanley, has some insight on a message about knowing God. He taught me a simple prayer that I have prayed a thousand times since this all happened: "God, I want to know you more than I want to know answers to all my questions." As time has passed, the memory of those days still haunts me, but my need to know the *why* has diminished.

I've also found great comfort at the piano, playing songs I believe God has given me. At first the music was for me, but then I realized it was also for others. I have been told that it has brought peace to broken men who have and will question the goodness of God. My music literally is the beauty that has come out of my ashes. My music was birthed in the midst of my torment; yet it is used by God to bring peace to others—ironic, huh? I am learning more about how hard this no-matter-the-cost pledge really is. I am a walking testimony that in addition to the wounds in our lives, there is music—notes and harmonies—that have the power to heal and make holy.

—Pete Ohlin
www.nomatterthecost.com/Pete-Ohlin

8

God's Will and Won't

"Whoever does God's will is my brother."
—Mark 3:35

A Brother's Story

As the son of a preacher man, I've heard the phrase "God's will" throughout my life. It's a valid phrase, although it is frequently butchered by whoever's talking about it. People have justified everything from unplanned pregnancies to September 11 on God's will. I can't talk much about God's will anymore. But I can speak of God's won't. Almost seven years ago now, I resigned from a pastoral role I was in. I had been working alongside a good friend, but the bright balloons of "wouldn't it be great to work together" began to pop one by one. And when the last one popped, there was nothing to do but fall. Although the two of us publicly declared my setting out for new vistas as "God's will," I don't believe we knew what we were talking about; it just sounded good and we buttered it with some Bible verses so folks could swallow it. Maybe so we could too.

But it hurt. Bad. There was personal damage, family damage, collateral damage, and just plain damage. I wanted God to come in and save the day, but he said, "I won't. You're just gonna have to fall on this one." And so we did. I say "we" because there was one other "won't" that surfaced during that time—the still, small voice that said, "I won't let go of you. Just hang on." And now, years later, like the blind man who saw men as trees walking, I'm beginning to see that God's won't is really God's will although it didn't look like it at the time. I imagine Jesus wondered about God's will when he was nailed to that cross. And the still, small voice said, "I won't let go. Just hang on."

—John Blase

www.nomatterthecost.com/John-Blase

Submit. Mention that word in any church anywhere and I'll bet you money that the men in the room immediately recall Ephesians 5:22—"Wives, submit to your husbands." We like that one, don't we? But that's not the only place that word is used in Scripture. How about these verses?

Do not be stiff-necked, as your ancestors were; submit to the Lord.

—2 Chronicles 30:8

Submit to God and be at peace with him.

—Job 22:21

In all your ways submit to him, and he will make your paths straight.

—Proverbs 3:6

Submit yourselves, then, to God. Resist the devil, and he will flee from you.

—James 4:7

Sometimes we think the lines "Your Kingdom come, your will be done on earth as it is in heaven" is an admission. Not by a long shot; it's a submission. It's the same reality Jesus submitted to in the garden:

> They went to a place called Gethsemane, and Jesus said to his disciples, "Sit here while I pray." He took Peter, James and John along with him, and he began to be deeply distressed and troubled. "My soul is overwhelmed with sorrow to the point of death," he said to them. "Stay here and keep watch." Going a little farther, he fell to the ground and prayed that if possible the hour might pass from him. "Abba Father," he said, "everything is possible for you. Take this cup from me. Yet not what I will, but what you will."
>
> —Mark 14:32–36

I wish I could say that submission gets easier with age, but it doesn't. If a man tells you it does, he's a liar. What I do hope, however, is that my response time is getting better the older I get. I used to be reactive, lose my cool or temper or peace of mind, and usually spew on the people closest to me. But I'm learning to be a little less reactive and a little more responsive. My response to the crisis or trial or temptation or test is "Your will, not mine." But it's still hard. I remember Rich Mullins singing something about "shaking like a leaf."

One more thing. In my worst moments of quiet desperation, when the feeling of peace feels like a distant land, when praying the Lord's Prayer I pause at the line "Thy kingdom come." I no longer have hope that the *kingdom of man* will lead to freedom. The ways of this world just aren't working. Almost every day the news of the world feels heavy and daunting, and I wonder when man's kingdom will just collapse. The truth is that we Christians are strangers in a foreign land trying to see our way through a *kingdom of darkness*. When I pause at the hope of a kingdom of God, I long for a kingdom of peace and pray that it will come soon—very soon. If God's kingdom promises peace, sign me up. That kingdom is worth fighting for. He is our Prince of Peace.

9

Unity of the Brotherhood

Though one may be overpowered, two can defend
themselves.
A cord of three strands is not quickly broken.

—Ecclesiastes 4:12

One of the grandfathers in what has loosely been called "the men's movement" is Richard Rohr. His voice has spoken faithfully for well more than a decade to men both young and old. Portions of his energy early on were invested in the Rites of Passage retreats. Of the tokens given to commemorate the completion of the retreat, one was a T-shirt printed with this old Celtic proverb:

Never give a sword to a man who can't dance.

Here's my interpretation: A man must fight for something or someone other than just himself and his personal satisfaction. He has to know the meaning of love and commitment, sacrifice and courage, duty and perseverance. In other words, he has to be a part of something greater than himself—a noble cause. That man knows about joy, there is a unity to his life; he knows how to "dance." If not, he's just a boy with a sword causing pain and suffering and further division to all around him, and most certainly to himself. In fact, according to Merriam-Webster the opposite of "unity" is "violence."

In John's gospel, chapter 17, we have what is referred to as "the high priestly prayer." These words conclude the upper room discourse found in chapters 14–16. Jesus is praying to the Father, his Abba:

> "I am coming to you now, but I say these things while I am still in the world, so that they may have the full measure of my joy within them. I have given them your word and the world has hated them, for they are not of the world any more than I am of the world. My prayer is not that you take them out of the world but that you protect them from the evil one. They are not of the world, even as I am not of it. Sanctify them by the truth; your word is truth. As you sent me into the world, I have sent them into the world. For them I sanctify myself, that they too may be truly sanctified.
>
> "My prayer is not for them alone. I pray also for those who will believe in me through their message, that all of them may be one, Father, just as you are in me and I am in you. May they also be in us so that the world may believe that you have sent me. I have given them the glory that you gave me, that they may be one as we are one—I in them and you in me—so that they may be brought to complete unity. Then the world will know that you sent me and have loved them even as you have loved me."
>
> —John 17:13–23

Has it crossed your mind lately that Jesus is praying for you and me? Have you considered that he's interceding before the Father? But he's not praying we'll get a great parking spot at the airport or that our fantasy football team will win next weekend. No, Jesus is praying with one thing on his mind—unity, that we would be as one.

> Christ Jesus . . . is at the right hand of God and is also interceding for us.
>
> —Romans 8:34

And don't miss the reality that unity will be threatened because of the presence of the evil one in this world. Jesus desires us to have the same kind of close-knit relationship with the Father that he does. And the evidence of that unity will be a symbol so *the world will know,* and what will they know? That the Father loves us.

If there's one weakness I've seen over the last decade in working with men in the Church, it's unity. The belief still persists that a roomful of men where somebody prays and someone else cracks open the Bible is equal to a unified group of men. That's sad, not to mention completely nuts. Notice that Jesus was very focused in what he was asking for—that we would be *one.* Furthermore, the unity that Jesus prayed for will be a symbol of the love between the Son and the Father. One area where I believe we've missed it is that we've gotten our signs and symbols mixed up. Let me try to explain.

A sign points the way to something. I live along the Front Range of Colorado, and our interstate has recently been equipped with these large green digital displays that read "Denver—50 minutes" or "Colorado Springs—15 minutes." That sign is not "Denver" or "Breckenridge" but points to them. A symbol, on the other hand, contains a quality of what it represents. Jesus prayed that we would be one, symbolizing the unity between the Father and the Son. Our unity here on earth does not just point to that greater unity, but it actually contains a quality of it because Christ lives in us and he and the Father are one. And such unity, as sometimes flawed as it is, is a witness to the world—*"Then the world will know that you sent me and have loved them even as you have loved me."*

The front cover of this book contains a symbol at the very bottom—a sword-shaped Celtic cross surrounded by twelve circles. Far beyond a great graphic for a book cover, we've taken that symbol and created a ring out of it to represent the quality of unity in our Band of Brothers. There is significant symbolism in this ring, both in origin and design.

> After David had finished talking with Saul, Jonathan became one in spirit with David, and he loved him as himself. From that day Saul kept David with him and did not let him return home to his family. And Jonathan made a covenant with David because he loved him as himself. Jonathan took off the robe he was wearing and gave it to David, along with his tunic, and even his sword, his bow and his belt.
>
> —1 Samuel 18:1–4

This was not an obvious friendship—these guys grew up on two different sides of the tracks. Jonathan was a prince, a son of King Saul and rightful heir to the throne. In great contrast, David was a shepherd boy. He may have been wearing the filthy clothes of a sheepherder as he stood in the presence of royalty. But Jonathan was humble enough to have a lens for David's true identity. Jonathan didn't see a shepherd boy—he saw a future king. He saw a part of God's plan, and he was willing to submit to it.

Jonathan could see David's anointing—not his own—to be the future king of Israel. He must have trusted God for his own story. So he sealed his commitment to David and called out and commissioned David to live out his anointed calling by bestowing kingly gifts—his robe, tunic, sword, bow, and belt. He didn't give David a new and improved shepherd's staff; he gave him a sword. He didn't give him another sheep for his flock; he put a royal robe on his back. The gifts were bestowed to represent his love and loyalty to David; in a word—*unity*. Jonathan then spent much of his life fighting for David and risking his very life to achieve David's true heritage—even against the will of his own father, King Saul. Because of his humility, Jonathan is one of the greatest warriors who has ever lived.

Saul was quite jealous of David. After the defeat of Goliath, the nation's attention turned to this young shepherd boy. You could hear it in their songs:

> Saul has slain his thousands,
> and David his tens of thousands.

Instead of following in his father's footsteps and nursing a jealous heart, we find a friendship that was greater than the forces around it. Jonathan believed in David, and he was willing to fight for David's glorious purpose. It is an amazing motivation to be believed in, in spite of the dirty clothes we may wear.

If you see a man wearing a Band of Brothers ring, be assured he didn't purchase it for himself. These rings can only be given. Sometimes this happens in a ceremonial setting accompanied by words like these: *I give you this ring as a symbol of my belief in you. You are an image-bearer of God. I believe in your heritage and glorious purpose—no matter the sins you have committed. I have seen your true identity—you reflect God uniquely. I see in you a warrior and brother of Christ. I am certain that when God looks at you, he is proud. I want to stand by you and fight for your life and legacy. When you need a friend, I am here. I pray that one day we will celebrate victory together at the banquet feast in heaven. There is no obligation to wear this ring. And there is no expectation of anything in return.*

As for the design, it too is symbolic; it carries a quality of what it represents.

The Battle—The sword-shaped Celtic cross is a reminder that I have been born into a battle. Sins such as sexual lust, pride, and greed can be devastating to my mission. Yet I have the power in me—the Spirit of God—to overcome the world, the flesh, and the devil. The sword shape is also a reminder to pick up and wield the sword of the Spirit (the Bible) on a daily basis. If I engage in my noble cause for Christ, my scars will not be in vain, victory is certain, and the rewards will be eternal.

Surrender to Christ—When wearing the ring, my own flesh can be seen in the pierced cross as a reminder that I now will trust God unconditionally and will pick up and carry my cross daily as a warrior, follower, and brother of Christ my King.

Band of Brothers—The twelve bright spots in the midst of the dark circle remind me that just as Christ chose to surround himself with twelve other men, so too should I remember not to try to fight the battle alone.

God's View of Me—Most important, the transparency of the cross shows my own flesh and reminds me that when God looks at me he sees my sin only through the perspective and lens of Christ's finished work on my behalf. I am a free man living under God's new covenant.

Some of you may be thinking, *All right, Vance, you've got a man giving another man a ring. . . . Don't you think that's just a little odd, something that might send the wrong message? Couldn't it be something that creates division rather than this unity you're talking about?*

As fair as that question is, and it is, I still have to chuckle when I hear it. We've not had a single man refuse the gift of a ring from another man. If you recall, it was a ring that the Father gave to his prodigal son to welcome him home. Our desire is to welcome broken men home. And a man needs to be called into the Last Battle by another man, not by a woman. We need to be challenged from a Jonathan-like man who has been given a lens by God for our glorious purpose. Sometimes we care too much about sending a wrong message and don't care enough about doing the right thing. In this case, the right thing is encouraging, affirming, and challenging other men to live out the mission for which they were created.

Teach us to care and not to care.

—T. S. Eliot

We care about the unity of the brotherhood. We care about assisting God in rallying together his chosen army. We care about being ready for the end moments. We don't care about that other stuff.

87

"Any kingdom divided against itself will be ruined, and a house divided against itself will fall."

—Luke 11:17

A Band of Brothers. Just what is that? It's a small number of men committed to fighting alongside one another for the cause of Christ, no matter the cost. It's as simple and as difficult as that. For a brotherhood to not just survive but thrive, there must be an agreement: relationships with no secrets and no condemnation. As crafty as Satan is, there is always a common line to his attacks—divide and conquer. And if there's anything that can divide and defeat men, it's secrets and shame.

I believe the most effective way to forge a bond between men begins with the willingness to share your personal story. But there cannot be any secrets; it must be an honest telling. There is an infatuation these days with being raw and authentic, a tendency to spill our guts. However, many times, especially among Christian men, it is a collection of "rubber guts." In other words, falsehood, fabrication, lies, posing, saying the things people either want or expect to hear. I have a friend who told me of working with a well-known Christian businessman, a leader highly praised for his transparent living. However, the reality was that this man allowed others to see only what he wanted them to see, nothing more. As bracingly honest as his stories were, they were still a pile of rubber guts.

I've been involved in men's groups before, and many of them leaned toward being "accountability groups." I understand that phrase, but I don't like it. I start from square one by telling my story as honestly as I can at the time. My story represents who I am. It stays with me through eternity. I don't want a man listening for inconsistencies or theological drift. I just want a man to listen, no condemnation. I don't want an accountant; I want a brother. I remember when I finally felt truly broken after my affair—in a really good way, in a way that made me want to become a better man. It wasn't when I felt judgment from others. It was when people like Brent offered Christ's undeserved grace and chose to believe in and fight for the good in me.

> Therefore, there is now no condemnation for those who are in Christ Jesus.
>
> —Romans 8:1

> And [the saints] overcame [the accuser] because of the blood of the Lamb and because of *their testimony*.
>
> —Revelation 12:11 NASB (emphasis mine)

What do you think of when you hear the word *testimony*? A tense courtroom scene with a nervous witness? A sweaty convert in a tent revival? In some sense, those mental pictures are close to the truth. A testimony does come from a witness: This is what I saw, heard, felt. And the story often has a before and after feel to it. In both cases, though, the expectation is one of telling the truth, so help you God.

There is a bedrock truth that anchors our testimonies:

> For all have sinned and fall short of the glory of God.
>
> —Romans 3:23

If you were to research the Greek word for *all* you would find that it means—surprise—"all." So every man, regardless of where he came from, how much his net worth, if he's got a six-pack or a fat tire, if he won the Nobel Prize or lost his marriage, the truth is he fails to measure up. None of us do; no, not one.

There is a continual awareness of "being level" in a Band of Brothers. This is the reason we do not offer gold-colored rings in the Band of Brothers—only silver ones. We do not want one brother to wear a more expensive-looking ring than another brother. This is the reason at Arlington Cemetery all the tombstones look exactly the same, white crosses, regardless of rank; these fallen men lived and died as a Band of Brothers. We also are a Band of Brothers uniting for the Last Battle, not a hierarchy. This is an area where Satan (the accuser in Revelation 12:11) hammers hard; the lies are that my sins are worse than yours or your failure is more devastating than mine. Lies, all lies. Remember, in Romans 3:23 *all* means "all."

My wife and I were one of a small group of couples that met over a three-year period. As wonderful as it was, there was simply no way to share openly with the other men in mixed company. Men need other men; we've been created to battle shoulder to shoulder. There was one man in the group I sensed a kinship with; however, we didn't know one another's wounds, temptations, and disappointments. As God would have it, we happened to sit next to each other on a flight to Atlanta. During the three-hour trip, we both felt safe to share our real stories. It was powerful, resulting in a deep and authentic brotherhood that thrives to this day.

The men in my Band of Brothers group know that I struggle with anxiety and sexual temptation. That knowledge, gained by hearing my story again and again, helps them discern when to support, encourage, challenge, or correct. Even when their assistance hurts, "wounds from a sincere friend are better than many kisses from an enemy" (Proverbs 27:6

NLT). Don't miss that phrase "again and again." That's one of the characteristics of a brother; he listens to your story, even if you've told it a hundred times. Additionally, if we do feel a spiritual prompting to confront a brother, Scripture teaches us to do it only with *humility and gentleness* (Galatians 6:1). Although I often fail at this, I try to do a "humility and gentleness" check on my spirit before challenging a brother about a blind spot in his life.

Once you've been entrusted with another man's story, you're response-able. In other words, you're able to respond with help or caution based on his revelation of himself. For example, let's say I find out that one of my brothers is struggling with loneliness. I know, because of hearing his story, that loneliness is not just some struggle for him, it's an all-out assault. In that moment I am able to respond, to be responsible. If I choose not to respond, knowing what I do about my brother's story, I've decided to be irresponsible. Hearing a man's testimony is not a small thing—it's holy ground; it binds your life to his as one committed to watching his back.

In the great epic battle against evil in *The Lord of the Rings*, the leaders from all of Middle Earth met at Rivendell to discuss how to destroy the evil Ring and thus prevent it from getting into the hands of the evil leader Sauron. The cause of good in the world depended on the successful mission of the Ring being destroyed by throwing it into the fires of Mount Doom.

The wise Elf Lord Elrond, who understood the dangerous quest that faced them, first challenged the men, "You will unite or you will fall." But the men of Middle Earth, the elves, and the dwarves all argued at the council of Elrond about which one of them should take the Ring. Finally Frodo Baggins, the simple and humble hobbit, was compelled by fate to submit to his calling: "I will take it! I will take it!" But what's even more important, Frodo had the humility and wisdom to admit his shortcomings: "But I do not know the way!"

Gandalf, the mentor figure and wizard in the story, is immediately drawn by Frodo's humility to offer his assistance: "I will help you bear this burden, as long as it is yours to bear." Aragorn then joins in by offering his gifts to the mission: "By my life or death, if I can protect you, I will! You have my sword." Then immediately Legolas and Gimli are inspired to offer their unique and different strengths: "And you have my bow!" responded Legolas. "And my ax!" followed Gimli. And Sam, Frodo's wonderful and loyal hobbit friend, fiercely states: "Mr. Frodo is not going anywhere without me!" The result is a total of nine companions, the "Fellowship of the Ring," each offering themselves to the dangerous mission to destroy evil in the world. This Fellowship, or band, offers a wonderful illustration of a group of men uniting to accomplish something truly good and noble that could never have been achieved alone.

> In the heat of battle it ceases to be an idea for which we fight, or a flag. Rather, we fight for the man on our left, and we fight for the man on our right.
>
> —Jack Durrance's final speech, *The Four Feathers*

God has given all his saints the unique and powerful gifts and stories that will be used in the Last Battle to defeat evil, but only if those gifts and testimonies are united.

Selah

The psalmist uses that word: *Selah*. As best we can tell it means "to rest, pause, or take a breath." Let's take a breather for just a moment—a selah. I know I need it. As I write these words, a hurricane is threatening the East Coast, which was already hit by an earthquake that damaged the Washington Monument. The country is bracing itself for another presidential election year, and some are predicting a second recession, as if the first wasn't enough. Although I've never seen an episode, *Jersey Shore* is the most popular thing on television; this obviously says something about us as a people. A friend's wife just had surgery to remove a tumor wrapped around her spine, and I haven't even mentioned what's going on with my kids and my wife and me. My wife just found out that her mother passed away. Dear God. . . .

> I am a little hurt, but I am not slain;
> I will lay me down for to bleed awhile,
> Then I'll rise and fight with you again.
> —"Johnie Armstrong,"
> old Scottish ballad

I've never read Kierkegaard and don't intend to start. But I'm not beyond stealing a phrase of his from time to time. He has one I found the other day—"tranquilization by the trivial"—that made me pause. Have you ever seen a man who looked tranquilized? Maybe it was the man looking back at you in the mirror.

Among the many scenes I love from the movie *Braveheart* is that moment when William Wallace is offered a sedative to ease his upcoming torture. He takes it but later spits it out. It always reminds me of the scene from the life of the original warrior-poet—

> They came to a place called Golgotha (which means "the place of the skull"). There they offered Jesus wine to drink, mixed with gall; but after tasting it, he refused to drink it.
>
> —Matthew 27:33–34

Jesus and Wallace both chose to face whatever was coming with eyes wide open. They chose to be alert. They refused to be tranquilized. As you and I go through each day in this world full of more than we can handle, one of our greatest challenges is refusing to be tranquilized by the trivial or even the somewhat meaningful. We must be discerning.

> Join with me in suffering, like a good soldier of Christ Jesus. No one serving as a soldier gets entangled in civilian affairs, but rather tries to please his commanding officer.
>
> —2 Timothy 2:3–4

This does not mean we're not involved in civilian affairs; it means we refuse to become entangled in them. I believe it means we realize our total dependence on the commanding officer—the Father. He is the one who gives. And we receive, no matter the cost.

10

Give Us This Day

With a humble heart, on bended knee,
I'm begging you please, help me.

—Larry Gatlin, "Help Me"

A Brother's Story

Yeah, it's been a journey for me with career and provision for my family. My undergraduate degree was in environmental sciences, but just as I graduated from UC Santa Barbara, I went on the road for two years as a drummer for an organization called Living Sound and then for Twila Paris. I eventually came to a fork in the road: I had to make a choice between the road and studio life as a musician, or a more stable family life and career that could more easily provide for a wife and children. I chose the latter (sometimes with some regret), worked construction and retail, then married my wife and immediately headed to business school at Duke. After completing an MBA, I joined the corporate world and worked thirteen years with GTE (which became Verizon).

I think I always believed I'd go to seminary and work in ministry, so a Duke MBA and the corporate track were not in synch with who I believed I was deep inside. God richly revealed himself to me through those years, and I had a lot of growing up to do, but they also felt like desert wilderness years. Lots of grace and good things in those North Carolina years—five sons, well-paying job, great church, rich community, almost on autopilot in some ways! Then the Lord started speaking into both my wife's heart and mine at the same time about our future. Through prayer, advice, and counsel from our community, we uprooted our family of seven and went to Regent College in Vancouver, British Columbia—basically left the good life behind! From that point forward it has been a completely different story of dependence on God for so much of life. Near divorce twice with my wife; deep, hard issues with raising five boys; hard extended family conflicts—you name it and we've walked through it. And I can't even begin to describe the heartache, shame, and frustration of not being able to find suitable employment for many years. I had a good education, a good job history, and good contacts, yet I could not find a good job. Trying to exhibit patience and have trust in God while waiting several years for him to deliver a suitable job was brutal. I felt thwarted by God. But in all this I believe my wife and I have found a different form of health with each other and with God, one that's been through the crucible and has survived. We've discovered a spaciousness.

I look back on the North Carolina years and wonder, *Who was that man?* I like the man I am today much better. I've been beat up and spit out, but I've hung on for dear life to the hand of Jesus. I used to be confused by the term *abundant life*—I really, genuinely couldn't understand what that could look like. Now I know that abundance refers to living life fully with high highs and low lows, and recognizing that the Lord is with us in them all, day by day. I've learned to love space as much as time.

—Matt Dealy

We are preoccupied with time. If we could learn to
    love space as deeply
as we are now obsessed with time, we might discover
    a new meaning in
the phrase *to live like men.*

—Edward Abbey, *Desert Solitaire*

This is a book for the barely brave who've lived long enough to know. . . . This book began with that line; it gave shape to the intended audience. As I've thought about it a little, this book is also for rich men, but I'm not using that phrase literally. Let me try to explain. Here's the story:

As Jesus started on his way, a man ran up to him and fell on his knees before him. "Good teacher," he asked, "what must I do to inherit eternal life?"

"Why do you call me good?" Jesus answered. "No one is good—except God alone. You know the commandments: 'You shall not murder, you shall not commit adultery, you shall not steal, you shall not give false testimony, you shall not defraud, honor your father and mother.'"

"Teacher," he declared, "all these I have kept since I was a boy."

Jesus looked at him and loved him. "One thing you lack," he said. "Go, sell everything you have and give to the poor, and you will have treasure in heaven. Then come, follow me."

At this the man's face fell. He went away sad, because he had great wealth.

—Mark 10:17–31

Author Richard Rohr calls this a parable about the second half of life. You live the first half of your life working and striving to make a name for yourself, establishing your business, growing the company, or carving out a niche. All men experience this; it's what you do the first half of your life. But there comes a time, maybe around thirty-five to forty years old, when an invitation to something more comes your way. I have to tell you the invitation can take the form of anything on the spectrum—an exciting adventure, a new friendship, loss of a job, a debilitating illness, a sinful lifestyle, or the death of a parent. In a very real way my son's battle with cancer was my invitation.

When that time comes, and I believe it is always divinely ordered, a man is faced with a choice: (1) live out the second half of life like the first, only trying harder, or (2) give up everything and follow him. I've seen many men step into their late forties and early fifties and redouble their efforts at striving and establishing and growing and carving. They are some of the most cynical and bitter men I know. Why? The thought is usually attributed to Carl Jung: "We cannot live the afternoon of life according to the programme of life's morning."

But I like the way Bagger says it best.

If you haven't seen the film *The Legend of Bagger Vance*, I highly recommend it. If you have, then you recall it being the story of a man's life told around the metaphor of golf. The once proud young golfer Junah (played by Matt Damon) went off to war and came home broken. He returns home and is faced with a decision about living the rest of his life. Life is going to swallow him regardless, but he has the freedom to say *how* it's going to swallow him. A mysterious caddy named Bagger Vance (played by Will Smith) comes along with some wisdom. There is a young boy named Hardy who idolizes Junah and wants to help in his redemption, wants to see him win again. Here's the scene where Bagger Vance is teaching young Hardy about an "authentic swing" on the night before the great match:

> Right here is where this game is won. Right here on the green. First you got to see it. Sun gonna be here in the morning. Over there in the afternoon. Funny thing is, the blades of grass gonna follow the sun. The grain is gonna shift. That same putt . . . gonna go one way in the morning, the other in the afternoon. One way in the morning, the other in the afternoon.

That's essentially what Jesus was telling the rich man: "One way in the morning, the other in the afternoon. To follow me you've got to walk away from the things that have defined you and given you security so far. The afternoon is different, trust me." Do you remember the way Matt described it?

> Lots of grace and good things in those North Carolina years—five sons, well-paying job, great church, rich community, almost on autopilot in some ways! Then the Lord started speaking into both my wife's heart and mine at the same time about our future. Through prayer, advice, and counsel from our community, we uprooted our family of seven and went to Regent College in Vancouver, BC—basically left the good life behind! From that point forward it has been a completely different story of *dependence* on God for so much of life. (emphasis mine)

In his bestselling book *Halftime*, Bob Buford describes well the transition to the second half:

For me, the transition into the afternoon of life was a time for reordering my time and my treasure, for reconfiguring my values and my vision of what life could be. It represented more than a renewal; it was a new beginning. It was more than a reality check; it was a fresh and leisurely look into the holiest chamber of my own heart, affording me, at last, an opportunity to respond to my soul's deepest longings.

Learning to pray and live the line "give us this day our daily bread" is a movement from independence to dependence, from a man focused on *getting* to a man surrendered to *receiving*. The true saint is the twice-born man—a man who no longer greets each day with closed fists intent on acquiring, but with open hands humbled to asking. *Give us.*

We are not fond of kindness.

—Dan Allender

Years ago Dan Allender was speaking at a conference in Addis Ababa, Ethiopia. After the session, a good friend escorted Dan and his team to a home where an evening meal was planned. The house was located in what might be called the barrios, a place of extreme poverty. To their surprise and delight, the meal began at four in the afternoon and concluded about three in the morning, wave after wave of courses consisting of food and drink and conversation and laughing and singing and dancing—"an evening of utter enchantment . . . one I will never forget." As Dan talked of the grand nature of the meal, this was his friend's reply: "You have no idea." What he discovered was that the hosts had been working for three to five days preparing the meat; they had slaughtered some of their own livestock for that special meal. It slowly began to dawn as to the probable expense involved in the evening. Once again Dan's friend said, "You have no idea. That meal probably cost this family one-twelfth of their income for the entire year. They spent a month's worth to celebrate you."

What would your response be to such a gift? Dan described his as "fury"—an immediate internal anger that an Ethiopian family would spend a month's worth of their hard-earned money so that a well-to-do American could experience an extravagant meal. His thought was, *This is not fair; this is not right!* His friend, who knew him well, moved into Dan's personal space and whispered, "I know what you're thinking right now. You're trying to figure out how you can get the money back for them, how you can repay the gift. Don't you dare defame their gift! Suffer the kindness of God on your behalf!"

> "For the kingdom of heaven is like a landowner who went out early in the morning to hire workers for his vineyard. He agreed to pay them a denarius for the day and sent them into his vineyard.
>
> "About nine in the morning he went out and saw others standing in the marketplace doing nothing. He told them, 'You also go and work in my vineyard, and I will pay you whatever is right.' So they went.
>
> "He went out again about noon and about three in the afternoon and did the same thing. About five in the afternoon he went out and found still others standing around. He asked them, 'Why have you been standing here all day long doing nothing?'
>
> "'Because no one has hired us,' they answered.
>
> "He said to them, 'You also go and work in my vineyard.'"
>
> —Matthew 20:1–7

Do you remember how the story goes from there? When evening came, each worker was paid the same amount. There was no distinction between those who'd worked since early that morning and those who'd only worked since five in the afternoon. And the immediate response by the all-day laborers was like Dan Allender's—"This is not fair; this is not right!" That's usually the emphasis when this story is preached or taught; a lesson for the pharisaical about grace. But this is not a book for the pharisaical; this is a book for broken men. So I want to draw your attention to something else here.

When the landowner went out at five in the afternoon, he saw some men and asked why they were just standing around. They responded, "Because no one has hired us." And why had no one hired them? These men were the screw-ups, the ragamuffins, the ones who had no doubt messed up so many times it wasn't funny anymore. These men were cheaters, liars, thieves, those addicted to all the things that don't make for good, dependable workers. Yet the landowner said, "You can work for me." And he ends up paying the Johnny-come-latelies the same as the early birds.

When you're broken, you don't feel like you have anything good to offer. It's hard to ask for anything because you don't feel like you're worth anything. If someone were to offer you a gift, you'd probably respond with "I don't deserve this. This is not fair, this is not right." That is exactly what the Accuser wants us to believe, that somehow we've gone too far. But the Good Father looks at us and says, "You can work for me. It's not about your earthly categories of fair and right or the good and bad of what you have done. This is about my kingdom and the ruling principle of my mercy."

A part of our training in this Last Battle is asking for bread each day, a declaration of our total dependence on God and exercising our trust in him to provide. We may not always feel we deserve the kindness of God, but the call is to suffer it, accept it, take it. The saint is the man who walks in gratitude for the Father's daily bread.

Matt Dealy's Story Continued

As I expressed earlier, these ten years in Colorado have been far from easy. Although it has been a wonderful place to finish raising our boys as four of them have headed off to college and career, the hole in me that represents deep identification with work/career has lingered. Make no mistake, God has provided. We've hung on and pieced together work/career moves to keep our finances and family stable, and for me there is deep fulfillment in our location. The spacious beauty of Colorado speaks into my soul, although the haunting question "What are you going to do when you grow up?" has never been silenced.

Until perhaps now. At least, that voice is a lot quieter! Something miraculous happened in the summer of last year. I went to take a hike with a good brother up at Bear Trap Ranch, which is InterVarsity Christian Fellowship's retreat and training center in the mountains right behind Colorado Springs. While there, we learned that InterVarsity was looking for a ministry organization to take over ownership and be the new stewards of the ranch.

After five months of intense due diligence by InterVarsity and Foundation of the Heart (the nonprofit arm of our Band of Brothers ministry), we received InterVarsity's donation of Bear Trap Ranch. That's right. God (through InterVarsity) *gave* us a thirty-acre ranch to do Band of Brothers retreats and to serve other aspects of God's kingdom. In an amazing convergence of so many of the threads of my life (work, education and training, Christian camp experiences, key relationships, and heartfelt passion), I have become the new executive director for Bear Trap Ranch. There could not be a more perfect job for me. I just showed up to take a hike with a friend, and God broke through in a totally unexpected, unanticipated, unimaginable way. There are seasons when God can be wild in ways that feel harsh, but there are also seasons when he can be wild in ways that feel extravagant—overly abundant! Throughout the due diligence process of the donation of Bear Trap Ranch, we kept in our hearts and minds one image: open hands extended before us. In fact, the property God gave us has mountain peaks that appear to form an open hand—isn't this wild? Even though it was difficult to fathom such a gift, we chose to receive whatever God has for us. During this afternoon of my life, I've learned new ways to hold on for dear life to the hand of Jesus: space and time, patient following, hanging on, hands outstretched to God. Give us this day. . . .

www.nomatterthecost.com/Matt-Dealy

11

Forgive Us Our Trespasses

Radio personality Paul Harvey told the story of how Eskimo hunters once killed wolves: First, the Eskimo coats his knife blade with animal blood and allows it to freeze. Then he adds another layer of blood and allows that to freeze, repeating this again and again until the blade is completely concealed by frozen blood. Next, he fixes the knife in the ground with the blade up. A wolf follows his sensitive nose to the source of the scent, discovers the bait, licks it, tastes the blood, and begins to lick faster and faster. The animal's craving is so intense that he does not realize the sting of the blade on his own tongue nor the instant when his thirst begins to be satisfied by his own blood.

I first heard this story retold from my friend Dave Dravecky. We refer to it as "licking the blade."

A Brother's Story

It was the fall of 2005. It was a great time in my life. I was on top of the world: beautiful wife, two lovely little girls, and the subject matter expert for an international nonprofit. That's how it looked from the outside. On the inside I was exhausted from travel, scared of competitive up-and-comers, and utterly alone. But I believed I could figure out the problems on my inside; after all, that's who I was, I figured things out.

It was also *my* fall in 2005. One day I delivered a grand vision speech to a roomful of colleagues. I had them eating out of the palm of my hand. After I concluded, my assistant approached me: "Matt, you rocked! That was amazing! I've never heard someone present like that!" In that moment I started licking the blade. My assistant's compliment was like blood to a hungry wolf. I began a year-long affair with a woman who also happened to be my wife's best friend. The affair probably would have continued but I got caught. I immediately began to try to figure the situation out because that's who I am, that's what I do. But I'd lost too much blood by then. My heartbroken wife told me, "You've forfeited your right to live in this house. Get your things and leave." I drove to a parking lot, grabbed my cell phone, and started to call a friend. It was then I realized I did not have a single male friend I could talk to, not one. I spent that first night in my vehicle, all alone.

—Matt Neigh

I've been trying to get down
To the heart of the matter . . .
But I think it's about forgiveness.
—Don Henley,
Michael Campbell,
John David Souther

Give us daily bread. But man does not live by bread alone, right? So forgive us. I believe forgiveness stands at the center of living a life of strength and honor "no matter the cost." It's as if everything builds to this line in the prayer; you can almost feel it coming, almost like everything in this Last Battle may hinge on forgiveness.

The evangelical preachers I grew up listening to had a basic outline for their sermons: three points and a poem. If you've experienced that, then you know what I'm talking about. If you haven't, don't worry. I'm going to follow that form here, not because I'm trying to preach but because I believe it's a good way to approach the heart of the matter. Those preachers also often used alliteration for their three points, each one beginning with the letter *A* or *T* or *R*. I'm not going to do that. But I am going to make it easy.

Here it is.

1. I'm Sorry
2. I'm Sorry
3. I'm Sorry
4. a poem

1. I'm Sorry

The older you get, the more you feel your humanity. Whether it's knees that can predict the rain or multiple trips to the bathroom at night, you realize you're not invincible. And unless you're completely asleep at the wheel, you also realize those weaknesses that have little to do with joints or bladders. I'm talking about our sorry-ness. For me, sexual temptation is an ongoing struggle. When it comes to that, I'm pretty sorry. All the evidence out there indicates I'm not alone in that struggle. We're living a life that doesn't fit.

> Therefore be imitators of God as dear children. And walk in love, as Christ also has loved us and given Himself for us, an offering and a sacrifice to God for a sweet-smelling aroma.
> But fornication and all uncleanness or covetousness, let it not even be named among you, *as is fitting for saints*; neither filthiness, nor foolish talking, nor coarse jesting, which are not fitting, but rather giving of thanks. For this you know, that no fornicator, unclean person, nor covetous man, who is an idolater, has any inheritance in the kingdom of Christ and God. Let no one deceive you with empty words, for because of these things the wrath of God comes upon the sons of disobedience. Therefore do not be partakers with them.
>
> —Ephesians 5:1–7 NKJV (emphasis mine)

I began chapter two with these words: *Friends warned me, but I was a blind fool. I am a sheep that was led to the slaughter.* As I reflect on that season in my life, it all started out so innocent. I was traveling a lot for work, primarily showing up for trade shows. I really didn't think it would hurt anyone to look at inappropriate movies or magazines in the privacy of my hotel room when I traveled. And the flirtations on the trade show floor seemed harmless enough. But as the sin became more pronounced in my life, I experienced a gradual estrangement from God. It was much like the fabled "frog in the kettle" illustration, where the frog is placed in cold water, the heat is gradually increased, and the frog eventually boils to death without ever knowing what got him. You've heard that one, right? Evil is very patient. It starts out small, like an innocent smile in the hallway. Once you get over the guilt of "harmless" sins, it's so much easier to go on to the next step.

I thought I could get out at any time. I was like Tom Cruise's cocky character Maverick from the movie *Top Gun.* I was talented in my work and I like the adrenaline rush of breaking a few rules now and then. If you remember the movie, at one point Iceman told Maverick he was dangerous. Unfortunately it was not a compliment; he was "dangerous" to his own, not the enemy. Before I knew it, I crashed and burned. And since we don't live in a vacuum, there was collateral damage to my family, work associates, and friends—in a word, my world. The only glitch in that frog fable is that it's not true; the frog will try to find a way to jump out as the water gets hotter. I guess that means I was sorrier than a frog, because I was content to soak and stew in the sin.

I could list other "sins" that plague us as men, but I won't. We've all seen those lists, heard those sermons, read those books. This book is written for a man who's old enough to know the chinks in his armor. But I do mention sexual sin for this one reason—unlike the others, it's a sin against yourself. It's fairly common to hear that "sin is sin"—lust is no worse than greed or lying. I agree; sexual sin is not worse, but it is different. Paul the apostle speaks to this:

> Flee from sexual immorality. All other sins a person commits are outside the body, but whoever sins sexually sins against their own body.
>
> —1 Corinthians 6:18

Before I sinned against the other woman, my wife, my kids, or my friends, I sinned against my own body, myself, the only "me" there is. The majority of us would never consider committing suicide, but sexual sin is a form of suicide. It may not be as immediate or final, but sexual sin is taking your own life a little bit at a time—"licking the blade." I'm sad when I think about a wolf dying in that way; this majestic creature reduced to a carcass in the snow. It's sad when a man, a majestic creation of God, is reduced in the same way.

Let's be real with each other. Like most men, we know that pornography and sexual enticements are being used by Satan against us. Evil has strategically invaded technology—especially the Internet. The Enemy's goal: destroy our hearts and minds, separate us from harnessing God's power, and crush our effectiveness as Christ-followers. Because of the high stakes in the Last Battle, the bar that our King gives his warriors in this arena is quite high. We are told to "stay away from all sexual sin" (1 Thessalonians 4:3 NLT) so that we can live in "holiness and honor" (verse 4 ESV). At the retreats that our Band of Brothers ministry conducts each year, we repeatedly hear that sexual temptation clearly is the nuclear warhead launched by Satan that causes men the greatest struggle. The Center for Bible Engagement (CBE), a research division of Back to the Bible, proved statistically that engaging God's Word (our sword of the Spirit) at least four times a week dramatically reduced a man's odds of viewing pornography. (For a detailed look at this topic, get your hands on the excellent book *Unstuck* by Arnie Cole and Michael Ross.) These findings from CBE shouldn't be all that surprising to us. Scripture teaches us,

> The word of God is alive and active. Sharper than any double-edged sword, it penetrates even to dividing soul and spirit, joints and marrow; it judges the thoughts and attitudes of the heart.
>
> —Hebrews 4:12

Although we know intuitively the additional value of walking in truth-telling brotherhood with other men, we commissioned CBE to conduct a similar study for the Band of Brothers ministry. The results were dramatic. In addition to engaging with Scripture most days of the week, building truth-telling relationships with other men reduced the odds of viewing pornography by *another* 31 percent! In other words, research proves that in order to become more like Christ and to be overcomers in the area of sexual sin, men must learn to wield the sword of the Spirit most every day and be side-by-side with other Christ-followers in true brotherhood. We believe these two weapons are the most important battle strategies for becoming a no-matter-the-cost warrior for our King.

Alone, I don't fight sexual temptation very well. I know that, it's been proven. So I rely heavily on the support and encouragement of my brothers to help me in that area. The difference in my life today is that I fight harder upstream, and I try to fight "in the light" and never alone. Whenever I fail in the sexual arena, I am committed to confess my sin within twenty-four hours to my brother Pete. I have a covenant with him to do so. And then we pray together. We pray for healing from the fall, and rely on the promise of the sword of the Spirit that tells us to "confess your sins to each other and pray for each other so that you may be healed" (James 5:16).

As my good friend Tim Pfeifer described, when we shine a light in the corner of a cave, the rats scurry—evil runs from the light. God understands how Satan uses our secret lives to take us out. When our King returns, "he will bring our darkest *secrets* to light and will reveal our private motives" (1 Corinthians 4:5 NLT, emphasis mine). Why wait? God's sword teaches that truth sets us free. Confessing our sins to a trusted brother helps remove the shame and guilt that hold us in bondage and make us ineffective in the Last Battle.

I want to make something very clear: I'm NOT talking about agreeing to some I'm-just-a-sorry-good-for-nothing attitude when we confess our sins; that's definitely what the accuser would like me to believe, but that's not true. The truth is that I am a child of God and a brother of Christ and a man made of flesh and blood who has sinned and will sin again.

> For I have the desire to do what is good, but I cannot carry it out. For I do not do the good I want to do, but the evil I do not want to do—this I keep on doing.
>
> —Romans 7:18–19

Evil would prefer that we stay down with our heads in the sand after we sin—again and again. The shame that Satan wants us to embrace is harsh. Jesus prefers that we get back up, again and again, and head north, again and again. I believe my fourteen-year-old son, Dylan, already gets this very important lesson. In his signature line in his email, he includes a quote from the movie *Batman Begins*. Thomas Wayne asks his son, "And why do we fall, Bruce? So we can learn to pick ourselves up."

In his book *The Great Divorce*, C. S. Lewis tells a great story about shame:

> Don't you remember on earth—there were those things too hot to touch with your finger but you could drink them all right? . . . If you will accept it—if you will drink the cup to the bottom—you will find it very nourishing: but try to do anything else with it and it scalds.

I'm a repeat prodigal, coming to the place where I can admit that in the light and still fight no matter the cost, and I believe this is a good and godly thing. I, for one, am so grateful for the blood of the Lamb and the freedom that his sacrifice gives me—again and again.

Please note that I am not talking about cheap grace here. It does matter in this war that we fight with all our might for purity and righteousness: "Seek first the kingdom of God *and His righteousness . . .*" (NKJV). It matters a lot. In this Last Battle we need God to be with us to be victorious. Scripture tells us to "seek good, not evil, that you may live. Then the Lord God Almighty *will be with you*" (Amos 5:14, emphasis mine). Remember the story of Gideon, when God said, "I am the Lord your God; do not worship the gods of the Amorites, in whose land you now live. *But you have not listened to me*" (Judges 6:10, emphasis mine). God is forming an obedient army, and he will demonstrate his greatest feats through pure vessels:

> In a wealthy home some utensils are made of gold and silver, and some are made of wood and clay. The expensive utensils are used for special occasions, and the cheap ones are for everyday use. If you keep yourself pure, you will be a special utensil for honorable use. Your life will be clean, and you will be ready for the Master to use you for every good work.
>
> —2 Timothy 2:20–21 NLT

Another prophetic book, Joel, gives us a glimpse into the army of obedient soldiers, the spiritual "navy seals" that God will use in the Last Battle:

> They charge like warriors; they scale walls like soldiers. They all march in line, not swerving from their course. They do not jostle each other; each marches straight ahead. They plunge through defenses without breaking ranks. . . . Before them the earth shakes, the heavens tremble, the sun and moon are darkened, and the stars no longer shine. The Lord thunders

at the head of his army . . . and mighty is the army that obeys his command.

—Joel 2:7–8, 10–11

I remember my mentor Brent giving me a great vision for why I want to fight for purity. He said, "Vance, this is not about biting the bullet to avoid sin. Of course there is grace for sin. This is about fighting for something better—fighting to be part of a story that will echo throughout eternity."

2. I'm Sorry

The phrase "Forgive us" is not a statement or a demand; it's a request. It's something that we ask for. It's crazy to think that God doesn't know what's going on in our lives if we don't ask or tell him. God knows our hearts (Psalm 44:21). So why do we need to ask? I don't know, I really don't. The best words I've found on this come from Annie Dillard's *Teaching a Stone to Talk*:

> Experience has taught the race that if knowledge of God is the end, then these habits of life are not the means but the condition in which the means operate. You do not have to do these things; not at all. God does not, I regret to report, give a hoot. You do not have to do these things—unless you want to know God. They work on you, not on him. You do not have to sit outside in the dark. If, however, you want to look at the stars, you will find that darkness is necessary. But the stars neither require nor demand it.

So maybe the discipline of asking for forgiveness ensures that I realize the gravity of my sin and how it weighs me down in this Last Battle. Maybe telling God "I'm sorry" means I truly care, that I give a hoot. But for some of us, confession rouses feelings of fear and punishment. Often these feelings have their source in the kind of earthly father you had. This is where the commitment to the Good Father shows itself, this is one of those places where you work toward seeing your earthly father now as a brother. "Our Father, who art in heaven" has a standard response to our admission of sin, one that evokes trust, one that repeat prodigals can depend on:

> "So he got up and went to his father.
> "But while he was still a long way off, his father saw him and was filled with compassion for him; he ran to his son, threw his arms around him and kissed him.
> "The son said to him, 'Father, I have sinned against heaven and against you. I am no longer worthy to be called your son.'
> "But the father said to his servants, 'Quick! Bring the best robe and put it on him. Put a ring on his finger and sandals on his feet. Bring the fattened calf and kill it. Let's have a feast and celebrate. For this son of mine was dead and is alive again; he was lost and is found.' So they began to celebrate."
>
> —Luke 15:20–24

If you don't get anything else out of this book, I pray you get this: God loves you. As my friend Kelly Williams preaches, "You cannot out-sin God's willingness and desire to forgive you." My wife, Betsy, is the wisest person I know. She once told me, "Vance, the internal battle is whether we choose to view God from the lens of love or the lens of fear. Choose love."

Our desire to feel God's love is another reason that I believe God wants us to share our testimony—all of it. He wants us to feel his love through his people. God put in our DNA a longing to be loved unconditionally. But if we have not confessed everything to those we love, the accuser

115

will cast that shadow of doubt, saying, "Sure, they say they love you, but if they only knew about *that sin* then there is no way they would love you." So at our core we desire not only to be loved, but to be *known* and loved. I want to be clear—it does matter where you've been and what you've done, who your parents were, the people you've helped or hurt, loved and lost. But what matters more is the Father's love. It is greater than our past, greater than our sin, even greater than our own hearts.

> If our hearts condemn us, we know that God is greater than our hearts, and he knows everything.
>
> —1 John 3:20

> For God did not send his Son into the world to condemn the world, but to save the world through him.
>
> —John 3:17

When Gideon finally repented of his sins, he built an altar to the Lord and named it Yahweh-Shalom, meaning "the Lord is peace" (Judges 6:24). God desires that we also experience peace from our confessions. He knows everything, and when we choose to turn back to him, he may not even let us finish our "I'm sorry" before he says "Quick! Bring the best . . . For this son of mine was dead and is alive again; he was lost and is found."

3. I'm Sorry

I know my sorry-ness. I believe in the freedom found in telling the Father "I'm sorry." And I must seek a similar freedom in saying "I'm sorry" to the one I've offended. And this is where it can get messy.

Boss Spearman: It's a pretty day for making things right.

Charley Waite: Well, enjoy it, 'cause once it starts, it's gonna be messy like nothing you've ever seen.

—*Open Range*

The phrase is most commonly translated in three ways:

Forgive us our *debts*.

Forgive us our *sins*.

Forgive us our *trespasses*.

As a boy who grew up watching westerns, I lean toward the last option. The word *debts* is usually associated with money. These days the word *sins* can mean anything or nothing at all. But the word *trespasses* has teeth to it, like the clearly marked sign—NO TRESPASSING—or the firm voice with the sawed-off shotgun in hand: "I don't take kindly to trespassing on my land!" The word means a line was crossed.

Jake walked over to Augustus. "I ain't no criminal, Gus," he said. "Dan's the only one that done anything. He shot that old man over there, and he killed them farmers. He shot Wilbarger and his men. Me and the other boys have killed nobody."

"We'll hang him for the killings and the rest of you for the horse theft, then," Augustus said. "Out in these parts the punishment's the same, as you well know.

"Ride with an outlaw, die with him," he added. "I admit it's a harsh code. But you rode on the other side long enough to know how it works. I'm sorry you crossed the line, though."

—Larry McMurtry, *Lonesome Dove*

I want to remind you of the foundational verse of the Band of Brothers—

117

And [the saints] overcame [the accuser] because of *the blood of the Lamb and* because of *their testimony.*

—Revelation 12:11 NASB (emphasis mine)

"Their testimony"—that's a phrase both deep and wide. It refers to a man's story, all of it, and if you're anything like me it includes the stories of making things right after you've crossed the line. It includes saying "I'm sorry" to those you've trespassed against. And that can be messy and hard and feel like death itself. But the Good Father loves to redeem and resurrect—remember that.

In April of last year, I made the decision to tell my children about my trespasses. Some of those sins would be mentioned in this book, and I wanted them to hear it from me before they saw something in print. I decided to begin by telling my older son, Collin. I sent out a request to my Band of Brothers, asking them to please pray for us and our time together. Collin was away at college, so I called and asked if we could meet. He agreed. I don't know when I've been so anxious.

The moments leading up to our time were heavy; they felt like death. I also could tell that Collin was nervous about the weight of it all. As I drove up to Fort Collins I phoned my parents. My mother offered needed encouragement: "Vance, there is power in our stories—as ugly as they may be." I agreed with her. After all, my story is all I have, and my only hope in life is that there is a path to redemption. For me, sharing with my son both the glory and the sorry-ness of my testimony felt like that path to take.

It's hard to find a place to eat in Fort Collins on a Friday night. Yet I prayed that we would find a place somewhere, as private as possible, but not so quiet that everyone could hear me talk. We ended up at a place neither of us had ever been to, nor even heard of. But as we arrived and were taken to our table, I knew that God answered my prayer—it was a perfect setting—the table had been set.

Before we began, Collin said, "Dad, I am not going to judge you." Those are the most freeing and powerful words I have ever heard. At that moment I knew that everything was going to be okay, that God was with us. Tears fell as I told my story, and much of the time Collin was teary-eyed, but I never felt any condemnation or judgment from him. Actually, Collin seemed appreciative. He saw from my story how pornography can ultimately lead to death. I'm grateful to be able to say that we've had many conversations/warnings about the addictive and destructive nature of this beast. After I finished, Collin said, "Dad, I have never allowed myself to be exposed to ANY pornography. I always understood the danger. Some of my friends have already been greatly harmed by it. But I knew to avoid it!"

Wow! I hardly had words. Could it be that at least some of my scars have not been in vain? Given Collin's battle with cancer and his valiant fight in the midst of this culture to shun pornography, I can only imagine how God is going to use this good man, my good son.

Out of death there is life and hope and love. Our time that night was one of the best and most meaningful times I have ever had with my firstborn son. Today I feel one step closer to God's larger story of redemption. I said I was sorry, no matter the cost. It was hard. It felt like death, and in some sense I believe it was. But it was good death.

Precious in the sight of the Lord is the death of His saints.

—Psalm 116:15 KJV

4. A Poem

> I said I'm sorry and a strange thing
> happened: I died, but not all of me.
> My ashes mixed with mercy
> and a stranger thing happened:
> I'm alive, no longer afraid to die.
>
> —J. B.

Matt Neigh's Story Continued

My wife told me she was considering divorce. She hadn't decided to, but it was an option. She said, "There's a men's group called Band of Brothers. They're having a weekend retreat soon and I think you should go." I was desperate to somehow salvage my marriage, so she could have suggested crawling on my hands and knees blindfolded across the country and I would have given it a try. I showed up not knowing what to expect, and the weekend was nothing like I expected. I shared my story with these men. I admitted my sorry-ness. Their response was not "Oh, everything will be all right" but "We're with you; let's work toward restoration. We will fight with you for your marriage, but even if it doesn't work out, we're with you." So I did. I began to fight for my marriage. The first step was telling my wife I was sorry in the deepest sense of that word.

My marriage has been on the mend for almost five years now. I am living in our home again, surrounded by my wife and two daughters. Is everything magically restored? No. It is better, but it's far from perfect. I still struggle with the same temptations I did back in 2005; in some ways I am the same man. What is different is best seen on the contact screen of my cell phone; it's a list of men I can call on regardless of time or day. I'm now fighting in this Last Battle alongside other men, brothers on my right and my left committed to my story in the larger Story. These are men who know my sorry-ness, but they also believe in my worth as a man, a husband, a father, and a friend. Instead of licking the blade, my brothers challenge me daily to swing the blade and fight, unafraid to die, no matter the cost.

—Matt Neigh

www.nomatterthecost.com/Matt-Neigh

12

Go the Distance

If you build it, he will come.
Ease his pain.
Go the distance.

—*Field of Dreams*

I started to have a chapter for the phrase "as we forgive those who trespass against us" and another chapter for the phrase "lead us not into temptation." But I decided not to because I'm afraid we might have missed something in taking a breath between the two instead of letting them flow right into one another. Here's my thought: We usually think about "lead us not into temptation" as a plea to be delivered from greed or anger or lust or something along those lines. But what precedes that phrase in the Lord's Prayer? A plea for forgiveness—both for our trespasses and those who have/are/will trespass against us.

What if the temptation we're praying to be led from is the temptation to not forgive those who trespass against us?

In other words, the temptation to withhold forgiveness. It's humbling to me that the only commentary that follows the Lord's Prayer are words that deal with forgiveness.

> For if you forgive other people when they sin against you, your heavenly Father will also forgive you. But if you do not forgive others their sins, your Father will not forgive your sins.
>
> —Matthew 6:14–15

What if, of all the temptations out there, and there are many, what if the greatest of these is to grit our teeth and clench our fists and refuse to extend the same mercy that we've been given? Because we can do that, can't we? We can refuse, and sometimes it gets more tempting as we get older. It may be one of the greatest challenges for a saint in the Last Battle, a battle that doesn't always look like broadswords and shrapnel. Sometimes it looks like baseball.

Field of Dreams is a movie about baseball. It's also a movie about sons and fathers and forgiveness. John Kinsella was once a minor league ballplayer. He had a son, Ray, and the tie that bound them together was baseball. But sometimes the son grows to hate the father's love. That was the story with Ray. He despised baseball by age ten. At fourteen, he refused to play catch with his dad. He had a huge fight with his father at seventeen and decided to leave home. Ray never looked back. John Kinsella died while his son was out finding his own way.

Fast-forward years later to Ray with a wife, a daughter, an Iowa cornfield, and a mysterious voice whispering, "If you build it, he will come." Ray is at that point in life where he realizes, if only slightly, that he can't live the afternoon like the morning, so he decides to follow this voice. First off, he plows under his corn and builds a baseball diamond. It makes about as much sense as Noah building an ark when there's not a cloud in the sky. Shoeless Joe Jackson and the other seven players banned from the 1919 World Series show up, and Ray thinks that must be what the voice was talking about. It was, but it wasn't.

Then a different message: Ray hears the voice say, "Ease his pain." Ray becomes obsessed trying to find out "who" and "what pain," so he sets out on a journey that leads him into the lives of other men and their stories and then eventually back to his own home and the ballfield he built in his Iowa cornfield. Shoeless Joe and his teammates are out playing a game, and when it's over, Joe speaks and points to the catcher: "If you build it, he will come." As the catcher removes his mask, Ray suddenly realizes it's his dad, young again, full of promise. Ray is confused with the message of "ease his pain" when Shoeless Joe says, "It was you, Ray." Ray's refusal to forgive his father had gradually eaten away his insides, particularly his heart. In a dramatic exchange that always gets me, Ray calls to his father, "Hey, Dad, wanna have a catch?" His father replies, "I'd like that." And the forgiveness is tossed back and forth in the form of a baseball, caught and thrown by a son and his father in a field where their deepest dreams came alive. The gloves are open, as are their hearts.

If only life was like Hollywood. It's not, but it is. It's not in the sense that emotional restorations like the one between Ray and John don't always happen, even when we do our best to re-create the mood or scene. But life is like that in the sense that our days are full of responsibilities and deadlines but there is always a voice saying, "If you'll forgive, I'll be there"

("If you build it, he will come"). The Father promises to be in that moment when against all common sense you open your hands and forgive the trespass or debt or sin. God promises his presence. He doesn't promise a Hollywood ending. The reality is yes, that might happen, but it's not promised. What is assured is that regardless of the outcome, the Father saw you go the distance and says, "Well done!"

In contrast to a field of dreams stands a field of reality. It's found in the concluding portion of a story you probably know well, maybe too well. Sometimes a familiar story causes us to shut off our brains a little. So that doesn't happen, here are those verses from *The Message* paraphrase of the Bible:

> "All this time his older son was out in the field. When the day's work was done he came in. As he approached the house, he heard the music and dancing. Calling over one of the houseboys, he asked what was going on. He told him, 'Your brother came home. Your father has ordered a feast—barbecued beef!—because he has him home safe and sound.'
>
> "The older brother stalked off in an angry *sulk* and *refused to join in*. His father came out and tried to talk to him, but he wouldn't listen. The son said, 'Look how many years I've stayed here serving you, never giving you one moment of grief, but have you ever thrown a party for me and my friends? Then this son of yours who has thrown away your money on whores shows up and you go all out with a feast!'"
>
> —Luke 15:25–30 THE MESSAGE (emphasis mine)

How many of you have perfected "the sulk"? A few clicks on the keyboard and Merriam-Webster tells me the definition is "moodily silent" and that the word comes from an obsolete word meaning "sluggish." Synonyms for *sulk* are *mopey, pouting, pouty, sullen, surly,* and *down-in-the-mouth.* I'll ask again—how many of you have perfected this?

In our twenties, we're still rank enough to yell and curse when we're wronged, maybe even throw a punch. By the time we're thirty we've settled a little and have a little more to lose, so we suck it up or suck it down when life doesn't go as planned. These are the days the seeds of sulk take root. Around forty or so, we've been betrayed or fired or divorced or overlooked for that promotion so many times that the seeds are now briars that tangle our feet and leave us "sluggish" in most every aspect of life. We put our heads down, dutifully do the work we're supposed to, and keep a "moodily silent" distance from those closest to us. There are numerous celebrations we're invited to and could be a part of, but we refuse to join in. We withhold forgiveness and find ourselves on the outside of life looking in.

So what's a man to do? Go the distance.

But what does that mean? Be a part of the revolution.

In his book *The Different Drum*, author M. Scott Peck encouraged something he called the Maundy Thursday Revolution. He considered the most important day of the church year to be Maundy Thursday, or the day before Jesus' crucifixion. This revolution has two stages. First, Jesus washed the feet of his disciples. Peck wrote:

> Until that moment the whole point of things had been for someone to get on top, and once he had gotten on top to stay on top or else attempt to get farther up. But here this man already on top—who was rabbi, teacher, master—suddenly got down on the bottom and began to wash the feet of his followers. In that one act Jesus symbolically overturned the whole social order.

The second stage is Jesus' gift of a new social order in the symbol of Communion, the secret of true community.

> When he had finished washing their feet, he put on his clothes and returned to his place. "Do you understand what I have done for you?" he asked them. "You call me 'Teacher' and 'Lord,' and rightly so, for that is what I am. Now that I, your Lord and Teacher, have washed your feet, you also should wash one another's feet. I have set you an example that you should do as I have done for you."
>
> —John 13:12–15

Jesus humbled himself and washed the feet of disciples who would soon betray him, scatter like the wind, and deny they even knew him. But he went the distance, no matter the cost, then said, "If you want to be a saint, then do as I did." I'm not diminishing the wrong that was done to you, but you can tight-fist that hurt for a lifetime and be a sulking, sluggish soldier in the Last Battle that needs alert, quick-footed warriors. At some point we've got to come in from the field of resentment and join the celebration, share a drink with a long-lost brother who has come home. We could even grab a glove and have a catch with the old man, or take a towel and wipe the spittle away from his mouth as he nears the end. Going the distance looks different for each of us, but all roads of forgiveness lead to the same place, a place with hands open to forgiving others their trespasses as we have been forgiven our own. A place where dreams come true.

A Story of Three Brothers

I was fired from our family business, by none other than my family. I couldn't believe it. Then to add injury to insult, my father sided with my brother, Keith. I believed I had done all the work expected of me, yet here he was standing with my brother against me. I hated both of them, I really did.

Even though I felt betrayed by Keith, and he felt badly wounded by me, we did agree to start praying for each other. For both of us, this was just an act of obedience to God. I was commanded by my King to pray for my enemy. A couple of years later Keith and I were driving down a road and I began sharing my testimony with him, my sins and failures, my affair, everything. My brother now had the ammunition to truly finish me off, the evidence that I really was the cockroach brother who deserved everything that happened. Instead, Keith pulled to the side of road, shut the car down, and began to weep. Then he started sharing his story, of how everything I thought I knew about wasn't really everything, wasn't the whole story. We embraced and wept and I forgave him as he forgave me. Two prodigals came in from their respective corners, we went the distance, and our pain was eased. The hatred and resentment dissolved, and now, twelve years later, my older brother is my biggest fan. And I'm his. Keith and I are connected with a spiritual bond that is difficult to fathom or explain. Our stories now are uniquely intertwined in bizarre and beautiful ways. Today, I love my brother with even more intensity than the hate I used to feel. Love really does win if we choose to be obedient to our King.

My dad is now eighty-two. With his hip problems he has trouble getting around at this elderly stage of life. This past summer he and my mother came out for my daughter, Noelle's, graduation from high school. Forgiving my father has been harder than forgiving my brother. We still don't agree about the right and wrong of what happened seventeen years ago, but I have realized that my hardheartedness toward my dad has caused many needless bruises. Recently I was able to hear some of my father's story. It's not my story, so I can't share it here. However, I began for the first time to see him more as a brother who has been badly wounded, bloodied by the same forces and struggles that have cut into me so deeply through the years. I saw that I am a "chip off the old block" when it comes to anxiety and fear. But I also saw a man who refuses to quit on God or life, in spite of the demons that relentlessly haunt him. That is the part of him that makes me proud to be his son. He has taught me how to fight until the end—in spite of life's difficult circumstances. I never want to be a quitter in this Last Battle. I want to be a man who always gets back up. And I believe I always will because I come from a determined bloodline. I am my father's son.

We didn't have a baseball, but we decided to go play tennis together. I was in awe to see my dad's tenacity hitting a tennis ball at his age—truly a force to be reckoned with, in spite of his poor health! But more important, our forgiveness was hit back and forth in the form of a tennis ball, back and forth by a son and his father who share many of the same battle scars. And although we hit from opposite sides of the court, we are a father and son who are on the same team. As we played, I began to embrace the many affirming and loving things my father has said to me over the years. I realized how much I love my dad and appreciate all he has done for me, in spite of the emotional torment he was facing through so many years. He does love me and is proud of the man I have become. I have often been too bitter to receive it . . . but not anymore. Satan's brilliant strategy of how to divide and conquer my family almost worked—but it didn't because of this amazing concept called forgiveness.

—Vance Brown

13

Humility
in the Mission

"I am sending you out like sheep among wolves.
Therefore be as shrewd as snakes and as innocent
as doves."

—Matthew 10:16

All right, let's rattle the cage a little. We've all heard that
Jesus is the Good Shepherd and we are the sheep of his
pasture and the Shepherd knows us by name and we know the
Shepherd's voice. Scripture presents that and I believe it. At
the same time, I confess those truths do little to inspire me.
Why? Listen to David James Duncan in his essay "Her Idiots":

They were her first flock or herd of any kind, her introduction
to shepherdhood. . . . And she expected to see some stupidity.
She'd been warned. She expected loveable ignorance, peren-
nial victimhood and a vacuous yet genuine innocence worth

the costs of feed and endless vigilance. But as she strode in past the mist, squatted beside an ancient ewe and met for the first time that direct, all-uncomprehending gaze, she was astounded: nothing had prepared her for such unspeakable nonintelligence. The eyes were hideous. . . . They understood nothing, never had nor would. Their seeing was not perception, it was radar—a cold, bloodless means of determining locations of meaningless objects.

Sheep. Idiots.

And in his classic *Of Wolves and Men*, Barry Lopez writes:

What happens when a wolf wanders into a flock of sheep and kills twenty or thirty of them in apparent compulsion is perhaps not so much slaughter as a failure on the part of the sheep to communicate anything at all—resistance, mutual respect, appropriateness—to the wolf. The wolf . . . is met with ignorance.

Sheep. Ignorant.

Again, I hold to the biblical imagery but I can't let it end there, not with sheep. Fortunately, Christ doesn't either. He knows the stakes that are involved in the Last Battle, and sheep don't stand a chance, unless something changes. Humility is needed; not a sheepish naïveté, but a shrewd innocence.

HUMILITY = SHREWD + INNOCENT

Much of what passes for humility in the church today is nothing more than weakness. You've seen it too. It's no doubt one of the reasons many men struggle so much with church. The virtue of humility is held up as an ideal, but it always feels soft. We've all heard the definition of humility as "bridled strength," but that always feels more "bridled" than "strong." The heyday of the men's movement saw a

131

renewed interest in learning to live shrewdly, to not always rush the field but to be cunning, crafty even. The problem for many, though, was the lack of "innocence," which often felt manipulative or just downright mean. Author Rick Lawrence defines these two words in his book *Shrewd*:

1. **Shrewdness**—Understanding how things work, then leveraging that knowledge to apply the right force in the right place at the right time.
2. **Innocence**—Freedom from guilt of any kind.

Shrewd as serpents and innocent as doves. When Jesus uses the word *snake* as a descriptor for shrewd, he's choosing the same word that, elsewhere in Scripture, describes Satan—in Hebrew it's *nahash*, the identical word Moses uses in Genesis 3:1 to describe God's enemy. And when he uses the word *dove* as a descriptor for innocence, he chooses the same word that, elsewhere in Scripture, describes the Holy Spirit. Jesus is saying, bluntly, that his disciples must be as shrewd as Satan is but not evil as Satan is. He's essentially telling us that we must beat Satan (and those in his service) at his own game by practicing a greater level of shrewdness than he does, but with none of his cruel intent or evil motivation.

That's the humility of a saint in the King's service. That's the humility crucial for your role in the Last Battle. Our Father wants to help us play the game better than the enemy. The best way for me to describe this is to tell you about a particular old sheep dog named Cymro—the best dog in a Welsh valley, an old dog, broke but shrewd in the service of his master. The story comes from David Whyte's *Crossing the Unknown Sea*. Cymro's owner, John, was widely known as a trainer of the very best sheep dogs. Many dogs had tried to best Cymro, but none were successful. Why? He never ran.

He never needed to, and besides, he was far too old to do it. When I first came to know this grizzled, one ear up, one ear down, black-and-white genius, he was about thirteen years old, virtually blind in one eye, with a distinct limp in his right hind leg. While other, younger dogs took off in the great curving runs up the sides of the mountain in order to move the sheep along, Cymro would simply limp behind the multitude of ragged backs and lean slightly toward them, showing the flock his good eye. With pinpoint accuracy, the sheep would pass straight through the gap in the wall where John wanted them to go. Cymro was a virtuoso, a Joe Montana of the dog world. He knew the pivotal places to stand, the pivotal ways to move; he occupied the center of the sheep universe and knew their collective minds even before they did; he barely ever broke into a lope. If I ever want to slow myself, I think of old Cymro's economy of presence.

The right touch or word at the right time in the right place. Energy and effort and will used only at pivotal moments. Shrewdness. Humility. It's the way for dogs and men who've lived long enough.

But there must be the presence of innocence or it's just manipulation; we must learn from the snake without becoming one. And how can I ensure that? It's a very trial-and-error journey, but at the heart is a daily dependence on God's Spirit, part of that "give us this day" line where we are constantly seeking the will of the Father. We will make mistakes along the way as we learn; that is inevitable. And in those moments we have the choice to say, "I'm sorry, forgive me." But as those moments build we become more and more humble, not some doormat but more like a stallion on a rein, powerful and strong but directed by the hands of our Father who is always near to us to accomplish what the Father wants. There is no formula or spreadsheet to this. It's about abiding in Christ, seeking first his kingdom and his righteousness. It's about faith and trust.

———

I remember well the exact moment I made my covenant with God to seek him first, regardless of the cost. It was May 16, 1999, the first anniversary of Brent's death. On that day I went back to the exact spot where his body finally came to rest in that rock canyon. I had come to another one of my George Bailey end-of-the-rope moments. After witnessing the tragic death of Brent, the man who I thought was going to help rescue me from my intense emotional anxiety and sexual addictions, I had continued to spiral that year. I felt completely broke—"not worth fixing." Yet it was in this state of wrecked desperation that I was finally ready to surrender my all—my Luke 14 "everything." I had no Plan B. Complete surrender to God was the only option that offered any hope. So I stood on the bank of the cliff deep in the mountains of Colorado and screamed:

I want everyone in the heavenly realms and unseen world to step up and hear what I have to say! That includes you, Satan, the demons under your command, the angels, the cloud of witnesses, and most importantly, my Father in heaven and the Trinity. At this moment I commit and covenant to follow Jesus my King, no matter the cost. So if it is your will, my King, that I die right now in this very spot like my friend Brent, then thy will be done. If it is your will that I stay on this earth and suffer for your glory, then thy will be done. But please don't let my suffering be in vain.

I'd love to tell you the heavens opened, peace washed over me, and I've lived happily ever after. I'd love to, but I can't. Instead, my anxiety and panic did not diminish for a long time. In hindsight, though, I *can* see that God honored my plea. Within a year, because of my emotional struggles, I resigned from my prestigious position as the CEO of a leading software company. At the time I felt immense shame; today I can see it was God's grace and mercy, part of his divine plan and desire that I leave. I could not understand God's goodness at the time. In fact, his will felt cruel. Today I can see that it was his goodness at work. My suffering was not in vain.

Making such a covenant with God feels scary, no doubt. What will my King ask of me? What burdens will he ask me to bear? What will it take to transform my heart and mind? But when I am at a good place spiritually, I understand my Father has my best interests at heart from his eternal perspective. Following him, no matter the cost, is what we were created to do—and it leads to ultimate peace and glory. It is the mission for which I was created. In fact, as we grow in Christ we come to understand that, in spite of life's circumstances, he is all we need and he is all we really want. Today I run another software company, but everything about it is very different, very redemptive. That is because I am very different.

In the years following my covenant with God in the canyon, I spent extensive time in prayer, in the Word, and with my family and brothers in an effort to detox from the hamster wheel of my corporate life. The Band of Brothers ministry was birthed out of these ashes. During that time some of my brothers and I crafted a covenant statement for the Band of Brothers that we believe helps to seal our cause and commitments—in other words, our individual and collective mission.

*I will surrender my all to God—no matter the cost—so that
I can become more like Jesus Christ—my brother and King. I
will seek out a Band of Brothers, for whose lives and legacies I*

will fight, so that together we can fulfill our mission to know, love and glorify God our Father.

Make vows to the Lord your God, and keep them.

—Psalm 76:11 NLT

Earlier I mentioned the ring that is engraved with the symbol for the Band of Brothers.

When a man first receives the gift of the ring from a brother and puts it on, the point of the cross faces his own body. This initial step is not necessarily symbolic. It simply means  that "some dude gave me a ring and spoke some words to me." However, it is given as a recognition of a man's own worth and a vision for his future glory if he accepts the call to engage in the Last Battle. Basically it is saying to a brother, "Yes, *it is about you*, and you have a unique part to play in this story that no one else was designed to accomplish." But at some point, and this is different in timing for every man, the recipient of the ring may voluntarily turn it around so the point faces out in the direction of other men and the world. It then is symbolic of one's own personal covenant with God to follow Christ unconditionally—no matter the cost. It is also a symbolic gesture that states, "As others fight for me, I will fight for others as well." Sometimes this "turning" occurs in a public setting, but more often than not it happens in a sacred moment between the man and God alone. That moment means something has changed—a wholeheartedness about seeking first the kingdom of God is being committed to—and the ring thereby serves as a monument to one's personal decision to sign up.

No one should take this commitment lightly. God will hold us to it. This is not a draft. The army God is rallying together during these monumental days for the Last Battle is made up of men who have lived long enough to have "considered the cost" and have made the decision to follow our King, even unto death.

It also hints at the reality that the intensity of the journey will increase; things will become more painful, but also more beautiful. This is the journey of sanctification. God will honor your covenant with him and you will be forged by your heavenly Father into a saint, a mighty warrior, the man you were created to be. There will be drudgery and waiting as God transforms our hearts and minds. Moses waited forty years from the time he was given a vision by God to free his people until the time it was fulfilled. Abraham and Sarah waited twenty years for their promise from God. Joseph spent many years in prison waiting on God's deliverance.

There will be ongoing temptations to not be faithful in our everyday ordinary living, in completing daily tasks that seemingly are the "small assignments." During this time God is training us and testing us to see if we are ready to take on more. Life often will feel crazy and lonely, and it will be hard to believe that "he is with us." In our sufferings and patience we will become more and more like Christ, our firstborn brother and the author and finisher of our faith.

If we are to share his glory, we must also share his suffering

—Romans 8:17 NLT

How impossible it is for us to understand his decisions and his ways! For who can know the Lord's thoughts? Who knows enough to give him advice? . . . For everything comes from him; everything exists by his power and is intended for his glory.

—Romans 11:33–34, 36 NLT

Let me be perfectly clear about this: Of course men can sign up to follow Christ unconditionally in true fellowship with other brothers without adopting this symbol or wearing a ring. We are not trying to hawk rings! In fact, all the profits from the rings and any other items we sell on our BandofBrothers.org site are donated to charitable kingdom causes. However, we are fighting to do our part to unite the clans for Christ, and our band has found this symbol to be a helpful reminder of our covenant with God. This symbol already has been trademarked in the United States and in many parts of the world to identify someone who has made a covenant to be a no-matter-the-cost follower of Christ.

When the battle gets intense and the fog and smoke hovers around us, a monument of our covenant with him serves as a beacon of light. It also helps to identify other brothers, other warriors, who have made the same commitment. It may sound like a small thing, but ask a man who wears the ring and he'll tell you: "Things changed when I committed to know, love, and glorify the Father."

To know, love, and glorify God our Father. But just what does that mean? Ask a room of twelve men and my bet is you'd get twelve answers. Here is how we define it: I recently came across some words that I believe reflect this mission in a memorable way. They're from a poem by Oliver Wendell Holmes titled "The Voiceless." I believe the lines reflect a deep-rooted feeling men know; we may not be aware of it all the time, but it haunts us. And I believe the lines give shape to our mission:

Alas for those who never sing,
But die with all their music in them.

Each man has a song in him. Robert Fulghum tells of standing before a group of kindergartners and asking, "Okay, who in this class can draw?" and everybody raised their hands. He asked, "Who can run fast?" and again, hands shot all over the room. He asked, "Who can sing?" and the air was full of childlike hands saying, "I can! I can!" Fulghum was in a classroom of college students not long after and posed the same questions: "Who can draw?" "Who can run fast?" "Who can sing?" Only the art majors raised their hands on the art question. The lettered athletes were the only ones who said, "I can run fast." And it was a select few of the music and theater majors who indicated they could sing. It made quite an impression on Fulghum. Futhermore, each of the specialists in singing or running raised their hands slowly, timidly, as if to say, "I can, but I'm not completely sure."

What happened between then and now? You can fill in that blank with the specifics of your life and your story, as I can mine. To some degree, all of our answers have a common thread—trying to be someone else.

Do you remember David wobbling around in Saul's armor?

David fastened on [Saul's] sword over the tunic and tried walking around, because he was not used to them.
"I cannot go in these," he said to Saul, "because I am not used to them." So he took them off.

—1 Samuel 17:39

We've all tried someone else's armor. That's part of it, trying and failing. But we've lived long enough to know "I cannot go in these." So I ask you—what's your song? What song must you sing with your life to sing the praises of your Creator? What were you created for? What is the part that you were born to play? If you want to think about it this way, what's your verse?

> In my class, you will learn to think for yourselves again. You will learn to savor words and languages. No matter what anybody tells you, words and ideas can change the world. I see that look in Mr. Pitts' eyes like nineteenth-century literature has nothing to do with going to business school or medical school, right? Maybe. You may agree and think yes, we should study our Mr. Pritcher and learn our rhyme and meter and go quietly about the business of achieving other ambitions. Well, I have a secret for you. Huddle up. . . . Huddle UP! We don't read and write poetry because it's cute. We read and write poetry because we are members of the human race. And the human race is filled with passion. Medicine, law, business—these are all noble pursuits necessary to sustain life. But poetry, beauty, romance, and love; these are what we stay alive for. To quote from Whitman: "Oh me! Oh life! of the question of these recurring. Of the endless trains of the faithless of cities fill'd with the foolish. . . . What good amid these, O me, O life. Answer: That you are here—that life exists and identity; That powerful play goes on and you may contribute a verse." The powerful play goes on and you may contribute a verse. What will your verse be?
>
> —*Dead Poets Society*

Our commitment is to stand alongside a man to make sure his voice is heard, to consider his role even more important than our own in the Last Battle, to fight shoulder to shoulder with him so he can contribute his verse to God's powerful play. We can know, love, and glorify our God by singing the song for him that we were created to sing and by encouraging our brothers to sing their songs also. Singing our songs

140

in unison is the only way we will win the Last Battle. The mission of the Band is to follow Christ no matter the cost and to fight for another man's song.

Let's revisit the story of Jonathan and David. In one of their last recorded times together, David "bowed down before Jonathan three times, with his face to the ground." They then "wept together—but David wept the most" (1 Samuel 20:41). David knew how Jonathan had saved his life and had fought for his story. David wouldn't have gone far without Jonathan. David's loyal brother later died in battle alongside his father, Saul. David became king, and he wrote a funeral song for Jonathan and Saul. He wanted Jonathan's story to be remembered forever, and he also obviously had forgiven Saul. As king, he "commanded" that the song be taught to all the people of Judah (2 Samuel 1:18). David was determined that his admiration for Saul and specifically his love for Jonathan would never be forgotten, and he was willing to use his power as king to make sure that everyone would remember their song:

> Oh, how the mighty heroes have fallen in battle!
> Jonathan lies dead on the hills.
> How I weep for you, my brother Jonathan!
> Oh, how much I loved you!
> —2 Samuel 1:25–26 NLT

This Jonathan-David story from Scripture where two men fight for each other's story, for each other's songs, is echoed in the movie *The Lord of the Rings: The Two Towers*:

Sam: I wonder if we'll ever be put into songs or tales.

Frodo: What?

Sam: I wonder if people will ever say, "Let's hear about Frodo and the Ring." And they'll say, "Yes, it's one of my favorite stories. Frodo was really courageous, wasn't he, Dad?" "Yes, my boy, the most famous of hobbits, and that's saying a lot."

Frodo: You've left out one of the chief characters: Sam Wise the brave. I want to hear more about Sam. [Frodo pauses, turns around, and looks deep into Sam's eyes and continues] . . . Frodo wouldn't have gone far without Sam.

Sam: Now, Mr. Frodo, you shouldn't be making fun. I was being serious.

Frodo: So was I.

A friend is someone who knows the song in your heart and can sing it back to you when you have forgotten the words.

—Bernard Metzler

> My heart, O God, is steadfast, my heart is steadfast;
> I will sing and make music.
> Awake, my soul! Awake, harp and lyre! I will awaken
> the dawn.
> I will praise you, Lord, among the nations; I will sing
> of you among the peoples.
>
> —Psalm 57:7–9

14

Deliver Us

Be alert and of sober mind. Your enemy the devil prowls around like a roaring lion looking for someone to devour.

—1 Peter 5:8

"Don't be afraid of the enemy! Remember the Lord, who is great and glorious, and fight for your brothers, your sons, your daughters, your wives, and your homes."

—Nehemiah 4:14 NLT

A Brother's Story

On the night before the death of my mentor Brent Curtis, I felt overwhelming oppression. I experienced intense fear and panic; I thought I was going crazy. Panic and anxiety had dogged me for years, but this was different. I sensed darkness all around me. I told Brent what was going on, so he gathered a couple of men to join us and pray. I was grateful for their efforts to rescue me, but the prayers didn't work. Or at least they didn't relieve my oppression. I tossed and turned all night long. I didn't sweat drops of blood, but I got real close.

The next day, as Brent and I took our "last walk" together through the canyon, I asked him what he thought about my panic the night before. Brent said matter-of-factly, "I could sense that you were being demonically attacked. Don't worry, we'll get through this together." In less than fifteen minutes, Brent fell to his death. In the weeks that followed Brent's death, my wife and I could feel intense oppression in our home. Our daughter was throwing up in her sleep. Our infant son was screaming uncontrollably at night. I felt completely helpless. I went on a search to find someone to help me fight the evil. I picked up a book on spiritual warfare and prayed every prayer in that book, word by word, line by line. But the resulting feeling was not deliverance but legalism. I was afraid to leave out a word here or miss a phrase there. It was a different kind of helplessness.

I learned about a man who was the "general" in spiritual warfare. He didn't live far away, so I visited him as quickly as our schedules allowed. At my first visit, he prayed a "warfare prayer" over me and told me to expect some relief. But the relief never came. In fact, after I got home I experienced one of the worst spiritual attacks of my life. The books didn't work; the general's prayer wasn't effective. What was I supposed to do? I had tried plans A, B, and C, yet nothing was working. I remember praying, "Dear God, I've had enough. Please let me die." In that moment, an image came over me. I was lying at the foot of the cross with my arms wrapped around its wooden base, and I heard, "My blood is your hope. I am sufficient! My blood is the only plan you need."

—Vance Brown

> They defeated [the accuser] through the *blood of the
> Lamb*
> and the bold word of their witness.
> They weren't in love with themselves;
> they were willing to die for Christ.
> Revelation 12:11 THE MESSAGE (emphasis mine)

People have asked me before what's different about Band of Brothers, what distinguishes it from other Christian men's groups or movements. We all build off one another, so there are some basic themes that sound the same. But when we get to this line in the Lord's Prayer—*deliver us from evil*—I believe one important difference emerges. It's what I experienced when I felt so oppressed and accused. I was frantic about messing up the words of the "warfare" prayers or anxious over what translation I used for which verse or nervous about where the prayer originated; it was exhausting. It was worry, plain and simple, and it did not bring an ounce of peace or freedom.

Now, don't get me wrong, I am not saying that warfare prayer is never appropriate, or that some people are not specifically gifted to engage in a special way. I believe it is and they are. But I am saying that it also can become legalistic and another form of bondage, and it has been blown way out of proportion. What I realized in that experience was that I was trying to get something started that had already been finished. *I* was trying to deliver me from evil, and that's God's job, not mine; he is the Rescuer and he must come—or as the apostle Paul says, "Woe to us." But Scripture gives us hope: "The Lord will rescue me from every evil attack and will bring me safely to his heavenly kingdom" (2 Timothy 4:18). He will work through us, especially his righteous warriors, in his timing. That's the prayer—*[Our Father] deliver us from evil*—and that's the deal. The pressure is off.

Author Larry Crabb is a guide for us here in moving from the old to the new:

> If the Christian life is all about blessings, then when trials come instead, we conclude either that we aren't living right or that God isn't really in control. In *this* situation, at least, Satan must enjoy the upper hand.
>
> When I developed cancer, I was told that it was from the devil and that I should engage in spiritual warfare against Satan on behalf of my health. The front line of spiritual warfare, in that view, is not to abandon myself to God in the middle of trial, but to align myself with God to defeat the devil. And the measure of victory is restored health.
>
> That, I believe, is the Old Way. In the New Way, we resist the fleshly demand that blessing replace trial and instead follow the Spirit, through whatever comes, into a deeper encounter with God. In the New Way we fight against the demand for blessings on behalf of knowing God.

The bottom line from Crabb is that the real battle is to abandon our demanding spirit to the good will of God, in spite of what bloody battles we may face. If we do, the pressure is off. That is in essence what we are saying by making a no-matter-the-cost commitment to follow Christ—when we do, the pressure is off. It now is up to him for us to live out what we were created for. We can't pull this off. As we are reminded, "Jesus *and the ones he makes holy* have the same Father. That is why Jesus is not ashamed to call them his brothers" (Hebrews 2:11 NLT, emphasis mine).

Whenever I felt intense spiritual oppression during those years with Brent, he would always ask me the question, "What do you think God is up to?" Instead of focusing on "what Satan is up to," Brent put more emphasis on the superior power and ultimate plan of our Deliverer. I believe if we are abandoned to his will, God will use our trials, tribulations, and pain (even when caused by Satan's hand) to conform us more into the image of his Son so that we can be used to accomplish great things in this Last Battle. We will live out what we are created for. We are free to sing our songs. That is the guarantee. And the guarantor is God the Father, maker of heaven and earth.

> The One who was born of God keeps them safe, and the evil one cannot harm them.
>
> —1 John 5:18

So then what is my job? To stand.

> Finally, be strong in the Lord and in his mighty power. Put on the full armor of God, so that you can *take your stand* against the devil's schemes. For our struggle is not against flesh and blood, but against the rulers, against the authorities, against the powers of this dark world and against the spiritual forces of evil in the heavenly realms. Therefore put on the full armor of God, so that when the day of evil comes, you may be able to *stand your ground*, and after you have done everything, *to stand. Stand firm* then, with the belt of truth buckled around your waist, with the breastplate of righteousness in place, and with your feet fitted with the readiness that comes from the gospel of peace. In addition to all this, take up the shield of faith, with which you can extinguish all the flaming arrows of the evil one. Take the helmet of salvation and the sword of the Spirit, which is the word of God.
>
> And pray in the Spirit on all occasions with all kinds of prayers and requests. With this in mind, be alert and always keep on praying for all the Lord's people.
>
> —Ephesians 6:10–18 (emphasis mine)

Satan is the great accuser, the master liar, in fact the Father of Lies. He knows the lies that have worked in my family line and the lies that work in yours. He will use them singularly or in any combination needed to achieve his desired result. He cares nothing about fairness or the Geneva Convention. His goal is condemnation, that we would condemn ourselves, one another, or worst of all, God. We all know the accusations will run the gamut and usually go straight for a jugular vein, right?

- If your Band of Brothers really knew how you satisfy your appetite for lust . . .
- Your wife's nothing but a frigid nag; she's always resented you.
- Your boss thinks you're weak; no, he actually knows you're weak.
- If God were good, why would he allow your loved one to suffer with sickness or die?
- You played by all the rules and your daughter still got pregnant.
- Real men rock climb, smoke cigars, and love sports. . . . That's not you, huh?
- The men in your church are all envious of you, which means they hate you.
- This is as good as it gets in life. . . . Sucks, doesn't it?
- Your best days are behind you.

Therefore, there is now no condemnation for those who are in Christ Jesus.

—Romans 8:1

That verse all too often stands in isolation. It is true and thank God it is, but what comes before it gives it context and life; it gives it blood.

What a wretched man I am! Who will rescue me from this body that is subject to death? Thanks be to *God, who delivers me through Jesus Christ our Lord!*

—Romans 7:24–25 (emphasis mine)

The accuser has no case against us—ever! My Deliverer and Rescuer is not me or some popular speaker or some well-crafted prayer, but the blood of the Lamb, Jesus Christ our Lord. Remember, "The Lord is faithful; he will strengthen you and protect you from the evil one" (2 Thessalonians 3:3). But Satan will raise hell to try to convince us otherwise. In those moments, and each day is full of them, our role is clear—stand. Put on every piece of armor there is, show up on the line, take the lies keeping your mind captive, and stand your ground. I could write paragraphs about the armor of God and what it is and what it means, but others have already done that and done it well. I want to draw your attention to two aspects of standing: where and how.

Where we stand is vital. The image I had in that horrible episode of oppression was that of holding on for dear life to the base of the cross, the place where the blood fell. There's no other place to take our stand other than at the foot of Christ's cross. If you're like me, I've exhausted most, if not all, of the other options by this point in my life. There's nothing left but the blood of the cross. The hymns of my youth drilled this into my head, and now, as an older man, they comfort and encourage my heart:

- "What can wash away my sin? Nothing but the blood of Jesus."
- "There is power, power, wonder-working power in the blood of the Lamb."

- "There is a fountain filled with blood, drawn from Immanuel's veins, and sinners plunged beneath that flood lose all their guilty stains."
- "My faith has found a resting place, not in device or creed; I trust the ever living One, His wounds for me shall plead."
- "Marvelous grace of our loving Lord, grace that exceeds our sin and our guilt! Yonder on Calvary's mount outpoured, there where the blood of the Lamb was spilt."
- "Redeemed, how I love to proclaim it! Redeemed by the blood of the Lamb."
- "Just as I am, without one plea, but that Thy blood was shed for me."
- "Though Satan should buffet, though trials should come, let this blest assurance control, that Christ hath regarded my helpless estate, and hath shed His own blood for my soul."

How we stand is just as important. The word used in Ephesians 6 is "firm." Stop and think about this a moment. Scripture doesn't say "stand hard" and it doesn't say "stand soft." But it does say "stand firm." I'm at that age where I believe strongly in joy, and one means to that end is pecan pie. Nobody likes pecan pie that's too soft, something you can't even pick up on a fork, something that runs away. In the same way, pecan pie that's too hard is usually sent back to the kitchen or thrown out for the crows to peck away; there's not a bit of joy in it. Pecan pie is at its best when it's firm.

As we pray "deliver us from evil," we have a responsibility—stand firm while waiting for the Rescuer. Running away soft is not the call for the saint. But neither is the hard-nosed militant charge-the-hill-for-Jesus. Some might think that's a moderate stance, just middle enough to be ineffective. Sorry, I don't buy it; I'm older now. It's a sober and humble stance, the way a saint stands. Steadfast. Constant. Dependable. Joyous. *Firm.*

I found tremendous relief when I abandoned myself to Jesus as my Deliverer. I also know that many men have found breakthrough by taking their stand against the Enemy and praying his attacks away. Both are called for. We need to surrender our demanding spirit to Jesus; but as men, we are also called to be warriors, and there is a place for spiritual warfare. As James said, "Submit yourselves, then, to God. Resist the devil, and he will flee from you" (James 4:7). First comes submission, total surrender. But then, from that place, we are commanded to resist. This is especially important for men. When my wife is under spiritual attack, it is my desire to first ask Jesus to come and deliver us. But then I believe I should take up my sword, and I pray for her. I want to do my part as I trust Jesus to do his. Finally, in the midst of those Gethsemane battles, I try to remember to pray like Jesus, "Yet not what I will, but what you will" (Mark 14:36). No matter the cost.

Also note the plural in that line—deliver *us* from evil. Applying that to the stance from Ephesians would mean that *we* must stand firm. That would mean there are days when I cannot stand on my own and I need a brother. That would mean there are days when my brother cannot stand on his own and he needs me. That would mean that being a Band of Brothers is what Christ had in mind when he said "Pray this way" or "This is what a saint's life looks like." A line of men standing firm, shoulder to shoulder, joy in their eyes, hearts not too soft and not too hard but just right, bloodied from the battle but also blood-stained from standing in the only place where it is and will be well with our souls—*there where the blood of the Lamb was spilt.*

The God of peace will soon crush Satan under your feet.

—Romans 16:20

15

All on the Field

Coach Eric Taylor: What do we tell our players
when they're facing a tough game?
Tim Riggins: Leave it all on the field.

—*Friday Night Lights*

Friday Night Lights is, in my friend John's opinion, one
of the best shows in television history. Expanding on
the hit feature film and bestselling book *Friday Night Lights*,
the award-winning show centers on life in Dillon, Texas,
where high school football brings the community together—
and the drama of small-town life threatens to tear it apart.
The pulse of the show is coach Eric Taylor, played by Kyle
Chandler. In a land of weak and stupid television fathers,
he is the exception to the fool's rule: strong, steadfast, firm.
Every pre-game speech ends with Coach Taylor's signature
phrase: "Clear eyes, full hearts." That's how they take the
field. And more often than not, the half-time locker room

speech includes another hallmark phrase: "Gentlemen, leave it all on the field." That's how they're encouraged to play the last half, holding nothing back, win or lose . . . *leave it all on the field.*

For Thine is the kingdom, the power and the glory, forever and ever. Amen.

The last phrase of the Lord's Prayer essentially says, "Men, leave it all on the field, for this is a fight worthy of your very lives." It is the banner that Christ will proclaim and wave during this Last Battle. It is the promise that will keep us going and inspire us to get up when we are injured or fall. That may sound odd at first, but let me explain. . . .

Two Brothers' Story

June 2, 2007

On the way home from church I asked Collin about the fear he experiences on a daily basis. "Dad, I didn't cause the cancer and I can't cure it. Sure, I get anxious, but at the end of the day it's in God's hands, so I'm not afraid." My son is enduring this rite of passage with a bravery beyond me. He knows the world can take his body but his soul belongs to God. Throughout most of my life I've been a fearful man—O me of little faith—so seeing my son's trust as he walks this valley of the shadow leaves me in awe. I've never had to face anything as monstrous as lymphoma. I've never had to bear up under the chemo and spinal taps. I've never been told my physical heart is weak or my blood levels are dangerously low. I've never had to face my mortality in this manner. But Collin is and he's facing it heroically.

It reminds me of one of my favorite scenes from *The Count of Monte Cristo*. It's a speech given over a son on his sixteenth birthday:

> Life is a storm. . . . You will bask in the sunlight one moment and be shattered on the rocks the next. What makes you a man is what you do when the storm comes. You must look into that storm and shout, "Do your worst, for I will do mine!" Then the fates will know you as we know you—a man!

Collin believes in God's kingdom and God's power and glory, forever and ever. Amen. And because of that faith he says, "Do your worst, cancer. I'm not afraid to die, because God is with me." After Collin's chemotherapy was completed, I had a desire that Collin would go back to playing high school basketball, a sport he had done so well in throughout his life. I thought returning to the game after battling cancer would be awesome, certainly an epic comeback story. After Collin's first time back on the court, he called me on the phone and said, "Dad, I realized today that I don't want to play basketball. I was doing that more for you than for me. I now realize life can be short, so I had better live my life. Instead, I want to play in a band with some of my friends." And what incredible friends he has! They all shaved their heads before Collin started his chemotherapy to show their support and love for him—a true Band of Brothers! In other words, Collin was saying, "I want to sing my song, not yours." That is when I knew my son was now a man. Unafraid to die, unafraid to live, and willing to trust God for his life story. About a month ago my friend Steve Metcalf gave Collin these words inscribed in a picture frame:

Collin,
Trust me.
I have everything
under control.
Jesus
—Vance Brown and Collin Brown
www.nomatterthecost.com/Collin-Brown

> They defeated [the accuser] through the blood of the
>   Lamb
> and the bold word of their witness.
> They weren't in love with themselves;
> *they were willing to die for Christ.*
>   Revelation 12:11 THE MESSAGE (emphasis mine)

I find myself writing this chapter on September 11, 2011, ten years after the terrorist attacks on U.S. soil. I don't claim to understand the terrorist mind and I don't know too much about religious extremists. But I do believe that on that day a decade ago, those men had a death wish, a desire for their own death as well as the death of others. That is not what Revelation 12:11 is talking about. In contrast, the New York City firemen had a life wish as they plunged into the smoke and rubble. Their desire was to save lives. They weren't looking to die themselves, but they were *willing* to die in order that others might live; they played to leave it all on the field. In my book, that's the difference between a soldier and a terrorist, between a thief and a savior.

> The thief comes only to steal and kill and destroy; I have
> come that they may have life, and have it to the full.
>
>   —John 10:10

I am a part of a small Band of Brothers. I assure you there's not one of us who wants to die. We love life and all that life has to offer. As fallen as this world is, it is still brimming with beauty. But we do stand shoulder to shoulder willing to die if that's what is needed for the cause of Christ. It might be a literal death like that of my friend and mentor Brent Curtis. And then it might be the daily deaths of dying to myself and my pride or my need to control or my cynicism. Regardless of literal or figurative, there is the willingness to die if that's what brings about life. Our commitment to such a willingness only exists because we believe in his kingdom and his power and glory. As Collin's plaque reads:

Trust me.
I have everything
under control.
Jesus

Trust. That's what it takes to pray and live the Lord's Prayer. That's what it takes to be a saint. That's what it takes to boldly share your story. That's what it takes to cling solely to the blood of the Lamb. That's what it takes to be willing to die no matter the cost. That's what it takes to receive daily bread, forgive others, and forgive yourself. Trust that he is the King, the Good Father, and it's his kingdom that's coming full of his power and for his glory and that nothing can separate us from his love. Trust. That's it.

The old hymn well summarizes the entire battle plan for the Last Battle: "Trust and obey, for there's no other way, to be happy in Jesus, but to trust and obey." The quote that follows is taken from the final journal entry of an unknown

Zimbabwean pastor martyred in the Last Battle. His are the words of a trusting man who left it all on the field:

> My future is secure. I am done with low living, small planning, smooth knees, mundane talking, chintzy giving and dwarfed goals. I no longer need preeminence, prosperity, position, promotion or popularity. I don't have to be right, first, tops, recognized, praised or rewarded. My face is set; my goal is sure. My road is narrow; my way is rough, my companions few. My God is reliable, my mission is clear. I cannot be bought, compromised, detoured, delayed or deluded. I will not flinch in the face of adversity, negotiate at the table of the enemy or meander in the maze of mediocrity. I am a disciple of Christ. I must go until He comes for His own, by the grace of God. He will have no problem recognizing me, because my colors are clear.

Some days are unforgettable: the day you get married, the days your children are born, the day you walk your daughter down the aisle. And then some days are about the kingdom and the power and the glory. They are days when you get what the old hymn writer called "foretastes of glory divine." Those days don't mean the battle is necessarily over, but they do cause you to cry "Yes!" On August 1, 2007, we received news from the oncologist that Collin's cancer was in remission. On that day we cried "Yes!" We experienced some of the *joy*.

> Therefore, since we are surrounded by such a great cloud of witnesses, let us throw off everything that hinders and the sin that so easily entangles. And let us run with perseverance the race marked out for us, fixing our eyes on Jesus, the pioneer and perfecter of faith. For the *joy* set before him he endured the cross, scorning its shame, and sat down at the right hand of the throne of God. Consider him who endured

such opposition from sinners, so that you will not grow weary and lose heart.

—Hebrews 12:1–3 (emphasis mine)

I'm not a theologian. I am a lawyer. But my friends who know about theological things tell me that the word *amen* basically means "Yes!" It's the battle call of the joyful, those who run with perseverance and endure whether it's cancer or bankruptcy or adultery or depression or the death of a friend. The saints rally their voices and cry "For Thine is the kingdom, and the power and the glory, forever and ever. Amen. Yes!"

My brothers, for the joy set before us, there's only one way to play the last half. Don't lose heart. Remember whose kingdom we're fighting for. Gentlemen, leave it all on the field!

Keep back nothing. Nothing that you have not given away will be really yours. Nothing in you that has not died will ever be raised from the dead.

—C. S. Lewis, *Mere Christianity*

THE END—

IT'S
ABOUT
HIM

I'm just a living legacy to the leader of the band.

—Dan Fogelberg, "Leader of the Band"

16

Great to Good

What he wished was not to be reckless, but brave,
a very different thing, and not to be mean but
proud, a different thing too.

—James Agee, *A Death in the Family*

A Brother's Story

August 29, 2011

We just learned that Betsy's mom, Mary, died. She and my
father-in-law, Paul, had been married sixty-seven years. According to Paul, his mission in life was to outlive his wife so he could
take care of her. Her health has been especially frail for the past
five years. He's done everything for her—cooked, cleaned, even
carried her from room to room—and always without complaint.
He spoke of her as an "angel" and did all that he could for her
right up to the very end. Paul is ninety-two years old. The look
on his face is now one of peace; he is sad, obviously, but there's

a peacefulness about him I can clearly see. And why? Well, because he lived out what he was created for—to love Mary, no matter the cost.

My father-in-law embodies the two brothers from *It's a Wonderful Life*. He fought the literal battles of WWII (like Harry Bailey) and he also fought the "battles of Bedford Falls" (like George Bailey). I am spending my afternoon of life trying to decide how best to be there for my wife, in this difficult moment and in others. Given all the wounds I have inflicted in her life, she deserves a good man. And what about my daughter, Noelle? I want to believe that there is a good man out there for her to marry. Just recently I was deeply moved as a father when I heard Noelle say, "I want to marry a good man, a man of God who would be a strong spiritual leader, a man who desires to serve the less fortunate, a man who is willing to be persecuted for the sake of his witness, a man who will fight to provide for his family—a man like Tim Tebow!" You can say what you will about all the Tebow-mania, but if he can influence my daughter to wait for a good man to marry, I will jump on the Tebow bandwagon! I do not know Tim Tebow and the kind of man he is when no one is watching, but unless I am willing to fight to be a good man myself, how can I expect that of others? I have a sterling example before me in the life of my father-in-law. I guess sometimes it is hard to find a good man, but not always. I know one personally; I've watched and hopefully learned from him. His name is Paul Johanon, and he is a good man. I want to be a man like that.

—Vance Brown

www.nomatterthecost.com/Paul-Johanon

I've read Jim Collins's book *Good to Great*. The book is fantastic in its approach and message. But I'm afraid a skewed version of that title has slipped into our Christian thought and polluted the waters. In our efforts to see a savior beyond the gentle, meek, and mild variety, I fear we've constructed a golden calf of the word *great*. But I ask you this—when God created the world way back there in Genesis, when all was said and done each day, what was his closing remark? "And it was great"? No, I'm pretty sure he used another word.

In the beginning God created the heavens and the earth. Now the earth was formless and empty, darkness was over the surface of the deep, and the Spirit of God was hovering over the waters. And God said, "Let there be light," and there was light. God saw that the light was *good*, and he separated the light from the darkness. God called the light "day," and the darkness he called "night." And there was evening, and there was morning—the first day. And God said, "Let there be a vault between the waters to separate water from water." So God made the vault and separated the water under the vault from the water above it. And it was so. God called the vault "sky." And there was evening, and there was morning—the second day.

And God said, "Let the water under the sky be gathered to one place, and let dry ground appear." And it was so. God called the dry ground "land," and the gathered waters he called "seas." And God saw that it was *good*. Then God said, "Let the land produce vegetation: seed-bearing plants and trees on the land that bear fruit with seed in it, according to their various kinds." And it was so. The land produced vegetation: plants bearing seed according to their kinds and trees bearing fruit with seed in it according to their kinds. And God saw that it was *good*.

—Genesis 1:1–12 (emphasis mine)

Not a page later and God said it wasn't *good* that man was alone, so along came the lady. Yeah, I'm thankful for that verse! The psalmist wrote that it is *good* and pleasant when brothers dwell together in unity (133:1). In Acts 10:38, Jesus himself is described as one who went about doing *good*. Even the word *gospel* describes news clarified by the word *good*. Don't forget the Bible itself used to be known as the *good* book. Why has this word that seems to mean such a great deal to God fallen on hard times? We've grown weary of good; we want the great, the epic, and the extraordinary. I don't know all the reasons why, but I wonder if God didn't intend for us to aim for great, but rather for good? What if he's quite delighted if we live good in this world gone bad?

I grew up reciting a lunchtime prayer that went something like this—

God is great,
God is good.
Let us thank Him
for our food.
Amen.

Maybe that childhood prayer was designed to teach us much more than just what to say before eating our sandwich. What if God is the only one who is both great and good? And what if we, his creation, were created to be good? We can't be both because we're not God. Maybe that was the temptation Lucifer couldn't resist; he tried to be both great and good, like God, but he slipped . . . and fell. Maybe the road to *great* is broad and wide, but the road to *good* is a knife edge you must be faithful to walk each day.

A phrase that's been heard for years is "A good man is hard to find." It feels like that sometimes among the men's groups I've been around. There are plenty of men striving for greatness, but few seeking to be good.

Love must be sincere. Hate what is evil; cling to what is good.
—Romans 12:9

Let us not become weary in doing good, for at the proper time we will reap a harvest if we do not give up.
—Galatians 6:9

Make sure that nobody pays back wrong for wrong, but always strive to do what is good for each other and for everyone else.
—1 Thessalonians 5:15

Dear friend, do not imitate what is evil but what is good. Anyone who does what is good is from God. Anyone who does what is evil has not seen God.
—3 John 1:11

Fight the good fight of the faith.
—1 Timothy 6:12

You may not remember the name James Agee, but you might have heard of his screenplays—*The Quiet One* and *The African Queen*—and his bestselling book *Let Us Now Praise Famous Men*. Agee was a writer and poet of considerable talent, spending the last years of his life working in Hollywood almost exclusively with John Huston. He died suddenly on May 16, 1955, at the age of forty-five. He had worked on another manuscript for years, and after his death his editors made sure it saw the light of day. *A Death in the Family* ended up winning the Pulitzer Prize in

1958. The story revolves around the death of a man, Jay: husband to Mary, father to Rufus and Catherine, and good man to many.

> Somehow I never got a chance to know Jay—your father—as well as I wish. I don't think he ever knew how much I thought of him. Well I thought the world of him, Rufus and Catherine. My own wife and son couldn't mean more to me I think . . . I always thought your father was a lot like Lincoln. I don't mean always getting ahead in the world. I mean a man. Some people get where they hope to in this world. Most of us don't. But there never was a man up against harder odds than your father. And there never was a man who tried harder, or hoped for more. I don't mean getting ahead. I mean the right things. He wanted a good life, and good understanding, for himself, for everybody. There never was a braver man than your father, or a man that was kinder, or more generous. They don't make them. All I wanted to tell you is, your father was one of the finest men that ever lived.

Eulogy. The word automatically conjures thoughts of a funeral or maybe a graveside service. A minister or family member, sometimes even a friend, is asked to deliver a *eulogy* for the deceased: It literally means "a good word." I approach that word a little loosely, so I feel it even means "a good story." If Christ does not return before your physical death, what will they say? Will they be able to share a good word or a good story about your life? Or will there be nervous glances by family members while the minister shares verses of comfort all the while avoiding how you lived your life?

———

There's a scene in the movie *Saving Private Ryan*. It comes late, almost near the end. The young private James Ryan, played by Matt Damon, is now an old veteran seen walking among the rows and rows of white crosses. He is visiting for the first time the grave of the man who made such a difference in his life, the leader who saved him—Captain Miller.

> Old James Ryan: [*addressing Captain Miller's grave*] My family is with me today. They wanted to come with me. To be honest with you, I wasn't sure how I'd feel coming back here. Every day I think about what you said to me that day on the bridge. I tried to live my life the best that I could. I hope that was enough. I hope that, at least in your eyes, I've earned what all of you have done for me.
>
> Ryan's wife: James? . . .
>
> [*looking at headstone*]
>
> Ryan's wife: Captain John H. Miller.
>
> Old James Ryan: Tell me I have led a good life.
>
> Ryan's wife: What?
>
> Old James Ryan: Tell me I'm a good man.
>
> Ryan's wife: You are.
>
> [*walks away*]
>
> Old James Ryan: [*stands back and salutes*]

That same challenge is before you and me, the dare to live a good life in a world gone bad. And the hope would be that our wives and sons and daughters and friends and neighbors would one day stand at our grave and say, "He was a good man." And then, in the lapse of eternity, we would stand before the Father and hopefully hear these words:

> "Well done, *good* and faithful servant."
>
> —Matthew 25:21

17

Dangerous Men

Let me tell you something, my friend. Hope is a dangerous thing.

—Red, *The Shawshank Redemption*

A Brother's Story

It was a story of epic assault, of epic odds set against us.

When Hadley was born, all her scores were normal. She did have a look about her, like she'd had a rough birth, but we just thought all babies look different. Ten days after her birth, we were back to the hospital and it was confirmed that Hadley had hearing loss. Okay, we can handle that. We went back at four months and her head hadn't grown at all. The doctor wanted to order an MRI and we agreed; we still thought everything was okay. I told my wife, Leith, "It'll be fine unless the doctor says he wants to see us in his office." The MRI was done on a Wednesday and our weekend was spent worry-free.

170

Then came Monday.

The doctor called Leith and said those words: "I'm going to need to see you and your husband in my office today." Leith calls me screaming, so much so I can barely understand her: "It's her brain! It's . . . her . . . brain!" What we found out in the doctor's office that day was that about 90 percent of Hadley's cerebellum was missing; it had simply never formed. She might be mildly retarded/disabled or she might require full-on care. It was like someone or something suddenly pushed us through a gate into a prison. It was our Shawshank.

There were moments when I'm sure it appeared we were fighting well, strong, and true. We did try. But there were just as many moments when our marriage held by a thread; times when we worried about our other two children and how Hadley's constant care affected them; and seasons of turning and turning the Rubik's Cube of God's will trying to match up the colors and discern what kind of story we'd fallen into.

For twelve years we anticipated the day Hadley would die. And then the day finally came. My daughter never spoke a word in her life. She never took a step. But her life touched continents of people with a wordless story of bravery and courage. And hope. My family and I stand here today afflicted but not crushed, perplexed but not despairing, persecuted but not forsaken, struck down but not destroyed. The enemy did not win. We are survivors. We are witnesses. Hope is a dangerous thing.

I miss her so much.

—Aaron McHugh
www.nomatterthecost.com/Aaron-McHugh

*T*he *Shawshank Redemption* is the film adaptation of a Stephen King novella. It tells the story of Andy

Dufresne, a man imprisoned for the murder of his wife and her lover. Although Andy maintains his innocence, he is sentenced to two consecutive life sentences at Shawshank State Penitentiary. He befriends "Red" Redding, an aging convict whose parole was recently rejected. In a gray place of routine despair and violence, Andy displays a virtue that gradually infects everyone around him. Andy is constant, steadfast, and firm. He literally chips away at his prison walls a little at a time, eventually finding himself facing his last and greatest challenge.

(Red narrating) In 1966, Andy Dufresne escaped from Shawshank prison. All they found of him was a muddy set of prison clothes, a bar of soap, and an old rock hammer . . . worn down to the nub. I remember thinking it would take a man six hundred years to tunnel through the wall with it. Old Andy did it in less than twenty. Oh, Andy loved geology. I imagine it appealed to his meticulous nature. An ice age here, million years of mountain-building there. Geology is the study of pressure and time. That's all it takes, really, pressure and time. . . . Turns out Andy's favorite hobby was totin' his wall out into the exercise yard, a handful at a time. . . . Andy crawled to freedom through five hundred yards of . . . foulness I can't even imagine, or maybe I just don't want to. Five hundred yards . . . that's the length of five football fields, just shy of half a mile.

Andy literally crawled to freedom against all odds, even when it meant trudging through almost half a mile of foul itself. I'm going to share three other short quotes from the film; each of them revolve around a certain four-letter word, a virtue that can make a man dangerous, no matter the cost.

172

Red: Let me tell you something, my friend. Hope is a dangerous thing. Hope can drive a man insane.

Andy: Remember, Red, hope is a good thing, maybe the best of things, and no good thing ever dies.

Red: I find I'm so excited, I can barely sit still or hold a thought in my head. I think it's the excitement only a free man can feel, a free man at the start of a long journey whose conclusion is uncertain. I hope I can make it across the border. I hope to see my friend and shake his hand. I hope the Pacific is as blue as it has been in my dreams. I hope.

In addition to striving to be a good man, I want to challenge you to be a man of hope. If you remember from the beginning of this book, that's the one thing George Bailey had lost—hope. It's hard, I know. It amazes me when I think of Aaron and the loss of Hadley and how brave this young husband and father is for holding on to hope in the face of such insurmountable odds. How is that even possible? I fall back on the words of a familiar hymn:

> My hope is built on nothing less
> Than Jesus' blood and righteousness;
> I dare not trust the sweetest frame,
> But wholly lean on Jesus' name.
> On Christ the solid rock, I stand;
> All other ground is sinking sand.

That familiar hymn falls back on the words of Scripture:

> Therefore, since we have been justified through faith, we have peace with God through our Lord Jesus Christ, through whom we have gained access by faith into this grace in which we now stand. And we boast in the *hope* of the glory of God. Not only so, but we also glory in our

sufferings, because we know that suffering produces perseverance; perseverance, character; and character, *hope*. And *hope* does not put us to shame, because God's love has been poured out into our hearts through the Holy Spirit, who has been given to us.

—Romans 5:1–5 (emphasis mine)

Though he slay me, yet will I *hope* in him.

—Job 13:15 (emphasis mine)

We all have our Shawshanks. Some of us have broken free. Some of us are still behind the bars. And some of us got out but found our way back in. I want to remind you of something I believe you know but which often gets buried in our world of routine despair and violence—hope is a good thing, maybe the best of things. And maybe today is the start of a long journey for you, but I hope you believe your conclusion is certain. A little pressure applied over time can make a huge difference. As a free man I hope you make it across the border. I hope to see you one day and shake your hand as a brother in Christ. And I hope heaven is as blue as it has been in my dreams. I hope.

Come to think of it, maybe that's what being a good man is—being a man of hope, one who never quits, one who keeps getting up, no matter the cost. So maybe my family members will one day stand at my grave and say, "Vance was a good man, a man of hope who never quit." I want to be a man who uses my story to bring hope to others so that my scars are not in vain. This would be redemption for me. I hope this for you too.

Be a dangerous man. Be a man of hope.

We will never come to embrace the heartache of our story until we see it profit another human being. Even then the sorrow doesn't leave, but seeing someone benefit from our pain adds hope to that pain, and our gratitude begins to transform our past.

—Dan Allender

18

We Happy Few

Then will he strip his sleeve and show his scars. . . .
This story shall the good man teach his son. . . .
From this day to the ending of the world,
But we in it shall be remember'd;
We few, we happy few, we *band of brothers*;
For he to-day that sheds his blood with me
shall be my brother.

—William Shakespeare, *Henry V* (emphasis mine)

I just returned from Washington, D.C., with my fourteen-year-old son, Dylan. For the past year we have been doing different quests and adventures with some other men and their sons as part of their "Passage to Manhood." Our favorite war monument was the one honoring the heroes from the Korean War, where it is inscribed "Freedom Is Not Free." Sure, the gift of salvation is free, but we still live in a world dominated by evil.

Of the saints that I plan to meet one of these days, Stephen is at the top of the list. His story takes up a few pages in the book of Acts and that's it. Acts 6 tells of the choosing of seven men to provide daily care for the believers so the disciples could devote themselves to the Word of God. One of the men they chose was Stephen, "a man full of faith and the Holy Spirit." He was one of those "good men," a man who was willing to "fight the good fight" behind the scenes administering a food plan for the poor and widows while the disciples were out teaching and preaching. During his seasons of being faithful in the "small assignments," God was preparing Stephen for a moment in time that would be a story to be remembered for all generations, a story that we talk and write about today. He has a story that parallels the story of Jesus and gives us hope that, as we are faithful in our small assignments, we actually can become more like him.

People started paying attention to Stephen due to his incessant speaking of Jesus of Nazareth. He was arrested, accused of blasphemy, and brought before the council and the high priest, yet Stephen did not varnish his speech:

"You men who are stiff-necked and uncircumcised in heart and ears are always resisting the Holy Spirit; you are doing just as your fathers did. Which one of the prophets did your fathers not persecute? They killed those who had previously announced the coming of the Righteous One, whose betrayers and murderers you have now become; you who received the law as ordained by angels, and yet did not keep it."

Now when they heard this, they were cut to the quick, and they began gnashing their teeth at him. But being full of the Holy Spirit, he gazed intently into heaven and saw the glory of God, and Jesus standing at the right hand of God; and he said, "Behold, I see the heavens opened up and the Son of Man standing at the right hand of God." But they cried out with a loud voice, and covered their ears and rushed at him with one impulse. When they had driven him out of the city, they began stoning him; and the witnesses laid aside their robes at the feet of a young man named Saul. They went on stoning Stephen as he called on the Lord and said, "Lord Jesus, receive my spirit!" Then falling on his knees, he cried out with a loud voice, "Lord, do not hold this sin against them!" Having said this, he fell asleep.

—Acts 7:51–60 NASB

Stephen was being stoned! Where was the Rescuer—the Deliverer? He was standing right there! A witness! In fact, he even stood up at the stoning of Stephen. This is the only place in Scripture that references Jesus standing at the right hand of God rather than sitting. I think Jesus was so proud of his brother Stephen that he could not just sit. That would be like sitting when your favorite player scores that winning touchdown for your favorite team in the Super Bowl. It's impossible to sit. You stand and cheer. Jesus was so proud that Stephen was living—and dying—according to the divine plan of their Father. Stephen didn't know until after his physical death how his scars would be used in the greater story. He didn't realize that because of his death the Christians would scatter in fear for their lives and how his death would begin the spread of the gospel throughout the world. Stephen's story will forever be remembered. I can't wait to one day meet Stephen and thank him.

Likewise, my mentor Brent Curtis did not know when he died that his book *The Sacred Romance,* coauthored with John Eldredge, would become a national bestseller. It had been released in 1997, before his death in 1998. Before he died, he told me about his disappointment that the book was not selling very well. Brent did not know before his death that he would be considered the father of the Band of Brothers ministry, and I can't imagine I would be writing this book if he had not believed in me at that crucial crossroad in my life. Brent could never have dreamed of the men's movement that was birthed with *Wild at Heart*. I'd be willing to bet that Jesus also was standing when Brent died. He was a good man. I can't wait to share all the stories with him on the other side. . . . I can't wait! But not yet. . . .

I told you early on I wouldn't trot out the rousing speech until it was time. Now it's time. If words or phrases here sound familiar that's because they are; they're taken from the very words of a young witness to the stoning of Stephen, a man named Saul who one day became that no-matter-the-cost apostle renamed Paul. I've often thought Paul got a firsthand lesson in what it truly meant to be a no-matter-the-cost follower of Christ when he stood and watched Stephen submit to the mob that day. He also learned something about mercy as Stephen cried aloud, "Lord, do no hold this against them!" Those words are reminiscent of Christ's from the cross: "Father, forgive them for they know not what they do." If we want to become like Christ, this is what it looks like. Sobering, huh?

Below I echo a paraphrased version of the words of Paul to you. They are found in different parts of Scripture, and I imagine they are words he spoke many times to rally men who were tired and discouraged. I speak them not as some muscular hero astride a white stallion with a soldier's armor covering my core. I don't live in the movies, but in the real world, a world full of terror and beauty. I speak these words to you a trembling and broken man, a brother barely brave but committed to serving my King—no matter the cost—alongside other brothers who've made the same decision. We are old enough to know our numbers may be few; in fact, we doubt it could ever be any other way. This is the narrow road. But we are also old enough to have experienced something rare in this life—happiness. Not some syrupy, shallow happy, but a deep contentment that comes from being on the Father's quest alongside a small fellowship, a happy few, a Band of Brothers. Men who will live out the purpose for which we were created. Men who will have an eternity of no regrets. Men who will have a cloud of witnesses cheering us on, with our Lord Jesus front and center.

The enemy will not win. We are survivors. We are witnesses. We are willing to shed our blood for our King, our brother. We are saints.

Hope is a dangerous thing. Remember the guarantee promised at the beginning of the book? It is worth repeating here. If you say "Yes, amen!" to Christ's call to live for him no matter the cost you will (1) live out the purpose for which you were created, (2) have an eternity filled with no regrets, and (3) have a cloud of witnesses cheering you on, including our Lord Jesus—our brother and King.

Brothers,

I beg you to live a life worthy of your calling, for you have been called by God. As Christ's brothers, do not get caught up in the affairs of this life. For we are not fighting against people made of flesh and blood, but against the evil rulers and authorities of the unseen world. And our old sinful nature loves to join this evil, which is just the opposite of what the Spirit in us wants. In this lifetime, we will never be free from this internal battle, but still we fight.

Don't be intimidated by our enemies. For if God is for us who can stand against us? For can anything ever separate us from God's love? No! Even the powers of hell can't keep

God's love away. For God did not spare even his own Son for us. So now there is no condemnation for those who belong to Christ Jesus. Once we were dead, doomed forever because of our many sins. Now God is working in us, giving us the desire and power to obey him.

We now have been called to live in freedom—not freedom to satisfy our sinful nature, but freedom to serve one another in love. For all of us together are Christ's body, and each one of us is a separate and necessary part. So let's encourage each other and build each other up, for we are in this fight together. So let's work together with one heart and purpose—and that's to bring others to Christ Jesus.

Brothers, you should know this, though. In the last days there will be very difficult times. So let's endure suffering as great warriors of Christ. Through suffering we constantly share in the death of Jesus so that the life of Jesus may be seen in us. Yes, we are pressed on every side by troubles, but we are not crushed. We are confused, but we don't give up. We are hunted down, but God never abandons us. We get knocked down, but we get up again and again and again and keep going.

We have learned not to rely on ourselves but on the Lord God, who will deliver us from every evil attack and will bring us safely to his heavenly kingdom. For we know that God causes everything to work together for the good of those who love him and are called according to his purpose. So be courageous and strong with the Lord's mighty power. For God has not given us a spirit of fear and timidity, but of power, love, and self-discipline. So let's fix our thoughts on what is true and honorable and right, and the Lord God of peace will be with us.

Brothers, let's keep our hope fixed on that day when we will finally be all that Christ Jesus saved us for and wants us to be. For God chose us to become like his Son, so that his Son would be the firstborn with many brothers. And having chosen us, he calls us to follow him. If we do, in the end we will say we have fought the good fight, we have finished the race, and we have remained faithful. And now the prize awaits us.

So let us bear on our bodies those scars that show we belong to Jesus. For us, to live is Christ, and dying is even better. If we die with him, we will also live with him forever. If we endure suffering for him, we will reign with him. For our present troubles are quite small and won't last very long. Yet they produce for us an immeasurably great glory that will last forever!

Men, we are more than conquerors. We can do anything through him who strengthens us; overwhelming victory shall be ours through Christ Jesus. Yet God forbid that we should boast about anything except the cross of our Lord Jesus Christ, for everything we accomplish is from him. At the name of Jesus every knee will bow and every tongue will confess that Jesus Christ is Lord and King, to the glory of God the Father. Amen.

The verse and question we began with still stand:

> They defeated [the accuser] through the blood of the
>   Lamb
> and the bold word of their witness.
> They weren't in love with themselves;
> they were willing to die for Christ.
>   —Revelation 12:11 THE MESSAGE

So, what say you?

*Will you be one of the saints used by
God to finally defeat evil . . .
no matter the cost?*

Epilogue

Yes, and I will continue to rejoice, for I know that through your prayers and God's provision of the Spirit of Jesus Christ what has happened to me will turn out for my deliverance.

—Philippians 1:18–19

I want to end this book by giving another nod to that classic film—*It's a Wonderful Life.* After the this-is-what-things-would-be-like-if-you'd-never-been-born segment, we find George back on the same bridge where his nightmare began, pleading with Clarence the angel:

Clarence! Clarence! Help me, Clarence! Get me back! Get me back. I don't care what happens to me! Get me back to my wife and kids! Help me, Clarence, please! Please! I wanna live again. I wanna live again. Please, God, let me live again.

Whether it's the battle of Bedford Falls or some literal overseas military campaign, the desire at the end of the day is always the same: *Get me back!* And that same image carries us into, through, and beyond the Last Battle. You can term it "deliverance" or "peace" or "heaven" or whatever you want to call it, but the word that encompasses them all is *home*. Why did Maximus fight the way he did? What was behind his willingness to strive against overwhelming odds? He wanted to go home. Why do those airport reunions between a soldier and his wife and kids cause even the hardest of hearts to melt with joy? The man came back; the prayers and yellow ribbons worked; he's home. And what did George Bailey long to return to, full of everything from Zuzu's petals to broken staircases to possible bankruptcy? Home.

Regardless of whether you had a good home, a poor home, or even if you've been homeless, that word and what it evokes is written deep in the marrow of our bones; it's a word of hope. Men, that is why we fight. That is why we keep getting up and trying again, even when the logical and sane thing to do would be to sit down and quit or drift off somewhere into the shadows. That is why we pray and live the daily prayer our Lord taught us and commit our lives to the Father and Jesus our King no matter the cost. It is the reward, a place he has prepared for us—home. I grew up with the understanding that one of these days we'd each have "a mansion just over the hilltop." Unfortunately that's a poor translation of Jesus' promise. He says: "In My Father's house are many rooms." Rather than some personal, isolated dwelling, think about it more like a grand family farmhouse with many rooms, one of them prepared for you. We'll all be together . . . all of us . . . home.

Once home, the veil is lifted once and for all and the confusion and craziness of our lives finally make sense. Our scars are monuments to bear witness to how the torment intended by the accuser was used by our Father for our good—our glory. Glasses are lifted and we laugh and tell stories about how God used our broken brothers, in the midst of their weakness and exhaustion, to swing their swords and sing their songs. The crowd of witnesses cheer and give testimony to how these mighty warriors harnessed God's strength and overwhelming power to restore his kingdom, and how they saw miracles that were even greater than those Christ had performed. At the homecoming feast and thereafter, we who said "Amen, yes!" are remembered—we few saints who were used by God to finally defeat evil. No regrets and no more tears. Redemption. Peace.

I also want to end this book by recalling that classic home-coming scene from God's Word, the story for broken men who've lived long enough. It is about a broken man coming to his senses with a twinge of memory, enough to stir homesick tears in the eyes of a pig-slopped prodigal and cause him to get up and step out of his moral and emotional filth. He remembered home. I'm going to take liberty with Scripture and paraphrase:

A Brother's Story

I was so far from home. The accusing voice in my head hissed "Maybe too far" but there was another voice, not much more than a whisper. It was my father's voice from too many days ago, a sad but firm declaration the day I took my inheritance and walked away: *"Remember: You're my son. You can always come home."* So clinging to nothing more than a memory, I, the broken man, got up, willed myself to hope, and repeated a single prayer: "Get me back." I didn't think things could get any worse, but with each step shame multiplied like rocks on my chest so that I could hardly breathe. Still a long way off I paused, doubting I could go any farther. The hiss in my ears was damning: "Too far." And then it was as if something from a dream, the whisper from my memory, a faint echo that only seemed to grow louder, almost like a song: "My son! My son!" Suddenly my starved bones were swept up by a goodness I recalled from long, long ago. As I looked up I saw my father's face, older now, streaked with homesick tears, but laughing like a boy. I started into my prepared confession but didn't make it past "Father, I have sinned . . ." as my father's voice drowned my shame with a mercy undeserved: "Remember: You're my son. Welcome home."

Then there was singing all around and over us, the songs of men unleashed, pure and piercing like the first snow of winter. And then it was as I had hoped—there was joy.

—a brother and son

And even those who were wild were singing a hymn that rose up to us on the mountain, and it was as though they marched in preparation for some imminent and joyous and sanctified war.

—Leif Enger, *Peace Like a River*

Six-Week Study Guide and Commitment

This book, including the following six-session guide, is intended as a resource for your journey as a man and as a training guide and preparation for engaging in the Last Battle. These materials can be used on your own—as a personal conversation between you and God—or as we are encouraging you to do, in a small-group setting. The six sessions will prompt you to consider your life honestly. We know how quickly the encouragement and camaraderie of discussing real-life issues with other men can be lost to the crazy demands of your world. We also know that you will be getting whispers from the Enemy. Satan does not want you to engage in this battle and unite with other men for the glory of our King, so please do not be surprised by many obstacles and reasons for not being part of a small group.

Accordingly, *we are asking you to commit to meet with some other men for only six sessions.* That's it! We recommend starting with six sessions and meeting *every* week together (not every other week). After the six sessions to-gether, you and your group can decide if additional meetings are desired. Some in the group may decide to exit, and this freedom should be gracefully extended. Others may decide to go to the next level of being in foxholes together, fighting for each others' stories in the daily battles and becoming a committed Band of Brothers.

(Note: If you are not ready, or for some reason do not have time to meet for six sessions with other men, you can engage with these questions online with other men at www .nomatterthecost.org. Please note that you must register with the site before the links below will take you directly to the online study questions.)

www.nomatterthecost.org/group/
no-matter-the-cost-book-study-questions

Basic Assumptions/Commitments

We hope you can approach these guided sessions in the following spirit: "The thoughts and themes of this journey together are those that reflect *a lifelong process*. I will consider these things at my own pace, and not at a pace dictated for me. I will be patient with myself and will not use this material to harshly judge or berate myself. When/if I go through this material in the company of other men, I will respect their pace and their own journey with God."

Where Am I Today?

An important question to ask is, "What level of honesty do I want with myself and God?" These guided sessions are designed to help peel away the layers of deception that we as men live under, so it is good to consider this question before beginning. These materials will be helpful only if you genuinely want more freedom, maturity, and love in your own life, and are willing to look at your life honestly in order to get there.

Using These Materials in a Men's Group

We recommend a group of four to six men. If your group is larger, we doubt there will be ample time for each man to openly and honestly engage with the questions. You probably should plan on meeting for two hours for each session. Assuming you are deciding to work through this material in a group setting, it would be good to determine some ground rules:

- **Group Leader**—Each group should have a leader to coordinate the meeting times, to send reminders to everyone each week about the assignments, to facilitate the times together, and to offer encouragement to the members of the group. The group leader also can be on the lookout for when meetings should be interrupted to intercede for a particular person in group prayer. The leader also should read ahead in the study guide to begin planning for the final ceremony.

- **Confidentiality**—Determine the parameters that you as a group wish to observe. For example, men's stories are their own to tell, and we believe those stories should be kept confidential. Accordingly, each person in the group should agree to not share another man's story with anyone else—including each person's wife.

- **Open or Closed Group**—Determine whether you want a "closed" group or you will be open to bringing other men into the group after it has begun. Because the original commitment is only for six sessions together, we recommend closed groups. Adding someone else in midstream when meeting for such a short time can be disruptive. After the first six sessions, the group can then decide whether to invite others into the group.

- **Confrontation**—Consider making a covenant allowing you freedom to speak into each others' lives. This will make it easier if things arise that need to be addressed. Implicit in this is that any confrontation will be done with respect and in a spirit of fighting for the other man with a spirit of *humility and gentleness*—not against him.

Before engaging with Week 1 questions in your small group or individually, please read the prologue and chapters 1 through 3. Each week, we also encourage you to read through and reflect on the questions before the group meeting.

Week 1 Questions

(related to the prologue and chapters 1–3)

The Beginning—It's About You

Opening Prayer

1. Describe past adventures you've taken, skipped, or missed. Are there any regrets?

2. Do you agree that in God's larger story, part of that story "is about you"? Why or why not?

3. Citing Revelation 12:11, the author suggests that God will use "the saints" to defeat evil and that the end days might be hastened if men would stop colluding with the evil one and "would band together, rise up, and fight shoulder to shoulder for the noble cause of Christ." What is your reaction to this assertion?

4. The author believes that God will use broken men in this epic battle. Why would God use broken men? Describe a time in your life when you can identify with the words: *all alone, exhausted, weary, bone-tired, questioning our worth, feeling much more dead than alive, courage struggling for oxygen.*

5. *What if* it was true that you had a vital role to play in the most important story in the history of mankind and that all your past scars would not be in vain? How could this change your life?

6. At the end of the prologue, the author sets forth a three-part "guaranteed" reward for making the commitment

to follow Christ "no matter the cost." What do you think about it? What if it's true?

Closing Prayer

For next time: Before engaging with Week 2 questions in your small group, please read chapters 4 through 9. We recommend reading one chapter each day and engaging with God about the content of each chapter on a daily basis. There are six chapters to read, so don't procrastinate! We also recommend reading beforehand the story of Gideon, found in Judges 6–8.

Week 2 Questions
(related to chapters 4–9)

The Middle—It's About Us

Opening Prayer

1. As you reflect on the question "Why has *this* happened to me?" describe the most significant battle in your life. Do you feel abandoned by God in the midst of this battle?

2. We are challenged to "seek first the Kingdom of God and his righteousness." If we do, we are given the promise that "all these things shall be added unto you." Describe what "all these things" could be in your life.

3. Romans 8:29 describes *God's purpose statement* for us, that we will "be conformed into the image of his son" and become Christ's "brother." In other words, we are being invited to be a "brother of Christ." How does that vision for your life make you feel?

4. Describe both the good and bad in your relationship with your earthly father. What is your view of God as "Father"?

5. Can you describe a time when things looked bad but later worked out for the better?

6. Scripture teaches, "In all your ways submit to him, and he will make your paths straight" (Proverbs 3:6). What are some areas in your life that you need to submit or surrender to God?

7. Do you have a relationship with another man where there are "no secrets and no condemnation"? Who, if anyone, truly sees you and believes in your glorious purpose? What are the pros and cons of such a relationship? If desired, how does one go about finding and cultivating such a relationship?

Closing Prayer

For next time: Sharing your testimonies. See instructions for Week 3.

Week 3

We recommend that this week guys take a *Selah* or pause from questions related to the book and take time to share their personal stories—their testimonies—with each other. This is an honest telling. Before the Week 3 meeting, each man should write out his story and prepare to read it to the group. Each written story should take about twenty minutes to read to the group. My friend Wes Roberts has a good format for doing this: You might begin your story by sharing your earliest memory. Then it can be good to organize your thoughts and memories according to the decades of your life. For example, you may want to share the three or four most significant positive experiences or memories from each decade and the three or four most difficult experiences or memories from each decade. It also is good to share the most impactful relationships—either positive or negative—from each decade. By writing out your story and keeping it to twenty minutes, it forces you to focus on the most significant life reflections.

For a group of six men to share, it will take around two hours. Please note that this is not the time to respond to each man's story. The goal is to simply share stories in a setting with no shame and no condemnation. Consider your meeting as a sacred place, hallowed ground, covered by the blood of the Lamb. Accordingly, at both the beginning and end of the time together, seal the time in prayer with the "blood of the Lamb."

For next time: Before engaging with Week 4 questions in your small group, please read chapters 10 through 15. Once again, this represents reading one chapter each day before the next meeting. We also recommend reading some of the story of Jonathan and David, which is found in 1 Samuel 18–20.

Week 4 Questions

(related to chapters 10–15)

Opening Prayer

1. In the first half of our lives we learn to be independent. But we cannot live the afternoon of our lives like the morning. How do you hope that the second half of your life will differ from the first half?

2. The Bible teaches us that God has a special use for those in his army who keep themselves pure (2 Timothy 2:20–21). Studies have shown that the most effective battle plan to overcome pornography and sexual addiction is to (a) engage with Scripture at least four times each week and (b) have truth-telling relationships with other brothers. Describe how you are wielding these two weapons in the battle.

3. The author states, "You cannot out-sin God's willingness and desire to forgive you." And the Bible teaches us that by confessing our sins to each other and praying for each other we can be healed and can experience peace. Are you carrying the weight of any sins in your life that have not been confessed to another person? Is there another person in your life you need to apologize to and seek his or her forgiveness? If there is someone in your life for whom you harbor bitterness and resentment, why have you not forgiven them?

4. What would it look like to live the life for which you were created? In other words, what song were you created to sing?

5. Describe times when you have felt tormented or oppressed by evil. Do you believe the Rescuer will come and will deliver you? Why or why not?

6. John 3:16 offers salvation to those who simply believe in his son, Jesus Christ our King. But have you ever made a Luke 14 covenant with God to follow this King unconditionally, no matter the cost? What would it take to trust God enough to make such a commitment?

Closing Prayer

For next time: Before engaging with Week 5 questions in your small group, please read chapters 16 through 18 and the epilogue. We also recommend reading beforehand the story of Stephen, found in Acts 6–7.

Week 5 Questions
(related to chapters 16–18 and the epilogue)

The End—It's About Him

Opening Prayer

1. Describe a man in your life that you would consider to be a "good man."

2. It is one thing to understand how there can be difficult consequences related to our intentional sin, but how can we trust that God is good when awful things happen to good people?

3. *"Hope is a dangerous thing."* Describe one of your deepest hopes and desires.

4. Stephen's scars and noble death can give us hope. How can your scars be used to give others hope?

5. Will you be one of the saints used by God to finally defeat evil?

6. Describe your vision of a *homecoming*.

Closing Prayer

For next time: Sharing in a ceremony. To prepare, see Week 6 instructions.

Week 6 Ceremony

Therefore encourage one another and build each other up.

—1 Thessalonians 5:11

During the last session together we encourage the group members to call each other out, challenge each other, and speak words of life to each other. Pray each day of the week before the final session together that God will give you a Jonathan-like lens for the other men in your group. Spend time listening to what is being spoken about each man in the heavenly realms. The hope is that each man will receive the anointed words spoken to him and will feel compelled to engage in the Last Battle, no matter the cost. There is no greater motivation to fight for purity and to "fight the good fight" than to be believed in, to be seen, and to be challenged to live out one's glorious purpose.

The group may decide to utilize a symbol to memorialize the final ceremony. You may also want to record the time together, so that the words spoken to each man are never forgotten. When the battle gets intense and the fog sets in, it is good to be reminded that our scars do not have to be in vain and that we do not want to miss out on our anointed roles in the larger story.

Finally, it is important to discuss whether or not men in the group want to continue meeting in some capacity. Men in the group should feel the freedom to no longer meet. There was only a six-week commitment to this particular study. However, some in the group may want to continue meeting and growing deeper in the relationships. Just remember, to be victorious in the Last Battle we cannot do it alone. To live out the purpose for which we were created, we need to be a part of Christ's true disciples, his Band of Brothers, and be willing to live or die for him—no matter the cost.

Notes

Foreword

pages 12–13   William Shakespeare, *Henry V*, 4.3. References are to act and scene.

Prologue

pages 18–19   Frank Capra, *It's a Wonderful Life*, directed by Frank Capra (1946: Liberty Films).

Chapter 1: What If?

page 26   David Whyte, "Sweet Darkness," in *River Flow: New and Selected Poems* (Langley, WA: Many Rivers Press, 2007), 348.

Chapter 2: Don't Go It Alone

page 32   Don Henley, "New York Minute," on *The End of the Innocence*, Geffen, 1989.

page 34   John Eldredge, *Wild at Heart* (Nashville: Thomas Nelson, 2001), introduction.

page 34   Ibid., 74.

Chapter 4: Courage for the Battle

page 48   Jim Uhls, *Fight Club*, directed by David Fincher (1999: Fox Studios).

page 50   Frederick Buechner, "The Two Battles," in *The Magnificent Defeat* (San Francisco: Harper & Row, 1966), 37–38.

Chapter 5: The F-Word

page 57   Charles Leavitt, *Blood Diamond*, directed by Edward Zwick (2006: Warner Brothers).

page 58   Robert Olen Butler, Twitter post, July 20, 2011, 2:28 p.m., http://twitter.com/#!/robtolenbutler.

page 61   William Gibson, *A Mass for the Dead* (Pleasantville, NY: Akadine Press, 1996), 253.

Chapter 6: Brothers

page 64   Henri Nouwen, *The Wounded Healer* (New York: Image Books, 1979), 99.

page 65   Robert Farrar Capon, *The Romance of the Word* (Grand Rapids, MI: Eerdmans, 1995), 98.

page 67   C. S. Lewis, *Mere Christianity* (New York: Macmillan, 1952), 45.

Chapter 7: Hallowed? Really?

pages 73–74   Capon, *Romance*, 221.
page 74   Ibid., 222.

Chapter 8: God's Will and Won't

page 79   Rich Mullins, "Hold Me, Jesus," on *A Liturgy, a Legacy, & a Ragamuffin Band*, Reunion, 1993.

Chapter 9: Unity of the Brotherhood

page 87   T. S. Eliot, *Ash Wednesday* (New York: Putnam, 1930), sect. 1.

pages 91–92   J. R. R. Tolkien, Fran Walsh, Phillipa Boyens, Peter Jackson, *The Lord of the Rings: The Fellowship of the Ring*, directed by Peter Jackson (2001: New Line Cinema).

page 92   Michael Schiffer, *The Four Feathers*, directed by Shekhar Kapur (2001: Paramount Pictures and Miramax Films).

Selah

page 93   Author unknown, "Johnie Armstrong," *The English and Scottish Popular Ballads*, ed. Francis James Childs, 169B.18.

Chapter 10: Give Us This Day

page 97   Edward Abbey, *Desert Solitaire* (Tucson: University of Arizona Press, 1988), 55.

page 98   Carl Jung, *Modern Man in Search of a Soul* (1933; repr. London and New York: Routledge, 2001), 111.

pages 98–99   Jeremy Leven, *The Legend of Bagger Vance*, directed by Robert Redford (2000: Allied Filmmakers).

page 100   Bob Buford, *Halftime* (Grand Rapids, MI: Zondervan, 1994), 31.

page 100   Dan Allender, *To Be Told* (Colorado Springs: Waterbrook, 2005), 180.

Chapter 11: Forgive Us Our Trespasses

page 106   Don Henley, Michael Campbell, John David Souther, "Heart of the Matter," on *The End of the Innocence*, Geffen, 1989.

page 110   Arnie Cole and Michael Ross, *Unstuck* (Minneapolis: Bethany House, 2012).

page 112   Christopher Nolan and David S. Goyer, *Batman Begins*, directed by Christopher Nolan (2005: Warner Brothers).

page 112   C. S. Lewis, *The Great Divorce* (New York: Macmillan, 1946), 61–62.

page 114   Annie Dillard, *Teaching a Stone to Talk* (New York: Harper and Row, 1982), 31.

page 117   Craig Storper, Lauran Paine, *Open Range*, directed by Kevin Costner (2003: Touchstone).

page 117   Larry McMurtry, *Lonesome Dove* (New York: Simon and Schuster, 1985), 572.

Chapter 12: Go the Distance

page 124   Phil Alden Robinson, *Field of Dreams*, directed by Phil Alden Robinson (1989: Universal Pictures).

page 126   M. Scott Peck, *The Different Drum* (New York: Touchstone, 1988), 293–294.

Chapter 13: Humility in the Mission

pages 130–131 David James Duncan, "Her Idiots" in *River Teeth* (New York: Dial Press, 2006), 15–16.

page 131   Barry Lopez, *Of Wolves and Men* (New York: Charles Scribner's Sons, 1978), 95.

page 132   Rick Lawrence, *Shrewd* (Colorado Springs: Cook, 2012), 31.

page 133   David Whyte, *Crossing the Unknown Sea* (New York: Riverhead Books, 2001), 121–122.

page 139   Oliver Wendell Holmes, "The Voiceless" in *The Illustrated Poems of Oliver Wendell Holmes* (Boston: Houghton Mifflin, 1885), http://name.umdl.umich.edu/ABX8133.0001.001.

page 139   Robert Fulghum, *Uh-Oh* (New York: Random House, 1991), 227–229.

page 140   Tom Schulman, *Dead Poets Society*, directed by Peter Weir (1989: Touchstone).

pages 141–142 Fran Walsh, *The Lord of the Rings: The Two Towers*, directed by Peter Jackson (2002: New Line Cinema).

page 142   This quote is sometimes attributed to C. S. Lewis, among others, but the best of our research leads us to believe it is original to the New York talk-radio host Bernard Metzler.

Chapter 14: Deliver Us

page 146 Larry Crabb, *The Pressure's Off* (Colorado Springs: Waterbrook, 2004), 84–85.

page 149 Robert Lowry, "Nothing but the Blood," 1876, public domain.

page 149 Lewis E. Jones, "There Is Power in the Blood," 1899, public domain.

page 150 William Cowper, "There Is a Fountain Filled With Blood," 1772, public domain.

page 150 Eliza E. Hewitt, "My Faith Has Found a Resting Place," 1891, public domain.

page 150 Julia H. Johnston, "Marvelous Grace of Our Loving Lord," 1911, public domain.

page 150 Fanny Crosby, "Redeemed, How I Love to Proclaim It!" 1882, public domain.

page 150 Charlotte Elliot, "Just As I Am, Without One Plea," 1835, public domain.

page 150 Horatio G. Spafford, "It Is Well With My Soul," 1873, public domain.

Chapter 15: All on the Field

page 155 Jay Wolpert, *The Count of Monte Cristo*, directed by Kevin Reynolds (2002: Touchstone).

page 157 John H. Sammis, "Trust and Obey," 1887, public domain.

page 159 Lewis, *Mere Christianity*, 191.

Chapter 16: Great to Good

page 168 James Agee, *A Death in the Family* (New York: Avon Books, 1959), 227–228.

page 169 Robert Rodat, *Saving Private Ryan*, directed by Steven Spielberg (1998: Amblin Entertainment).

Chapter 17: Dangerous Men

pages 172–173 Frank Darabont, *The Shawshank Redemption*, directed by Frank Darabont (1994: Castlerock Entertainment).

page 173 Edward Mote, "My Hope Is Built," 1834, public domain.

page 175 Allender, *To Be Told*, 180.

Epilogue

page 183 Capra, *It's a Wonderful Life*.

page 186 Leif Enger, *Peace Like a River* (New York: Grove Press, 2001), 304.

Vance Brown is chairman and CEO of Cherwell Software, Inc., a leading provider of service management software applications. Formerly, Vance was CEO of GoldMine Software Corporation (currently FrontRange Solutions). In 2009, Vance was given the "Entrepreneur of the Year" award by his alma mater, Wake Forest University.

A licensed attorney, Vance is also founder and chairman of the ministry Band of Brothers (www.BandofBrothers.org), which leads church conferences and provides small-group materials, online community forums, and technology designed to help men "fight the good fight." This ministry also hosted the Foundation Conference for business leaders (originally launched by Bob Buford and Bill Hybels) and currently owns and manages Bear Trap Ranch, a renowned training and retreat center in Colorado.

Vance and his wife, Betsy, live in Colorado Springs and have three children, Collin, Noelle, and Dylan.

John Blase is a writer and editor. His work includes the books *Touching Wonder* and *Start With Me*, and most recently he coauthored Brennan Manning's memoir, *All Is Grace*. John and his wife, Meredith, have three children and live in Monument, Colorado.

BAND OF BROTHERS
www.bandofbrothers.org

The purpose of the Band of Brothers Ministry is to offer the brotherhood of Christ to men fighting to move from success to meaning, addictions to freedom, and selfishness to God's call. Our Covenant with God is (1) to become a follower and brother of Christ—no matter the cost; and (2) to engage in the battle with other like-hearted men in authentic, secret-less relationships.

www.beartrapranch.org

Bear Trap Ranch is a world-renowned retreat center, now owned by the Band of Brothers Ministry, located just 30 minutes outside of the center of downtown Colorado Springs, Colorado. Once on the property there is a distinct sense of being truly remote–in a place of wonder, beauty, peacefulness and adventure with a deep sense of home. The vision for this property is that it become the premier training and retreat center for men who desire to follow Christ, no matter the cost.

nomatterthecost.org
an online community

Join thousands of other men online at www.nomatterthecost.org, our Band of Brothers' online community for men to connect with one another, form online groups, blog and share stories.

A Valuable Resource to Help You Live *No Matter the Cost*

A Proven Path to a Thriving Walk with Christ

Unstuck

🚦

Your Life, God's Design, Real Change.

Arnie Cole + Michael Ross

When asked about their relationship with God, many believers say the Christian life "isn't working" or that they want "more than an okay walk." After conducting extensive survey research on the topic, Back to the Bible leaders Arnie Cole and Michael Ross reveal the ways believers like you are growing—and thriving—spiritually. What's more, *Unstuck* gives you practical and proven ways to encounter Scripture daily, connect with God, and revitalize your faith.

Unstuck by Arnie Cole and Michael Ross

🕮 BETHANYHOUSE